WHAT TO DO
Before
"I DO"

PREPARING FOR THE
MARRIAGE OF YOUR DREAMS

HIAWATHA HEMPHILL

What to Do Before "I Do"
Preparing for the Marriage of Your Dreams

Hiawatha Hemphill
PLUANNA CITY PRESS
High Point, NC

PLUANNA CITY PRESS

ISBN: 978-0-692-06158-9

Extraordinary Praise for
What To Do Before, "I Do"

"The best books (and by this, I mean the most helpful) are usually filled with the personal experiences the author has had with victory and defeat. This book is a good read because its author satisfies these requirements. Hiawatha Hemphill pulls us to his side and invites us to walk with him through his singleness journey. His book contains a good deal of valuable information that will help singles live out their lives with joy and an expanded sense of purpose and peace."

—Dr. Ronald E. Hawkins
Vice President for Academic Affairs and Provost, Liberty University

"Singleness can be one of life's greatest challenges. Society's messages to singles are counterproductive to God's plan and create loads of unwanted confusion and hardship. So, what do you do if you don't know what to do? You read this book; it's loaded with biblical answers! Whether you are single or divorced and single again, *What to Do Before "I Do"* is a must read for you."

—Pastor Paul Kendall
Senior Pastor, Christ Family Church, host of *Family Matters*,
and author of *The Marriage Miracle*

"I encourage you to read *What to Do Before "I Do."* Hiawatha Hemphill has been a cherished friend for many years. As you read this book, his wisdom and practical insight will be a blessing to you. Although written with singles in mind, this resource will help heal your past and deepen your trust and dependence upon the Lord, regardless of your marital status. Thanks, Hiawatha, for your labor of love in producing this work."

—Dr. James Peoples
Pastor, Trinity Baptist, Keystone Heights, FL, and former President, Florida Baptist State Convention

"Rev. Hiawatha Hemphill's book provides practical and needed insights about why we must understand and love ourselves before we can deeply love a companion. His use of scripture-based detox affirmations and reality checks, and focus on development of the entire person make *What to Do Before "I Do"* a helpful, compact, quick-read guide.

"Rev. Hemphill's approach—to first unlearn our toxic past, then get ready for love—is a guidepost with next-step advice that helps with dating, marriage, and life in general. He gives the reader model prayers and practical advice that, if applied, can guide people to a loving Christian relationship with their spouses, and to salvation through Jesus Christ.

"I recommend this book to all who are serious about living their lives based on godly principles and wisdom, as these will lead them to establish and maintain long-term, healthy love relationships."

—John X. Miller
Senior editor, News and Commentary, ESPN
(John.Miller2@espn.com), Washington, DC, theundefeated.com

DEDICATION

I dedicate this book to:

Hannah, Luccity, and Plumie, the beautiful women who
lovingly raised me.

My little sister Pat. You are the best.

My extended family and friends.
My love for you transcends time and space.

My church family, Servant's Heart Worship Center.
You are a joy to serve.

My Lord and Savior Jesus Christ.
I love you more than life, because without you there is no life.

Special Thanks to Servant's Heart Worship Center Counsel
Members, Barney Charles Jones, Thomas Barclay,
Jim Kochenburger, Integrative Ink, Van-garde Imagery, Inc.,
Picture Perfect Photography, Boni Russell, and everyone who
played a role in making this book a reality.

CONTENTS

PREFACE

They told me when I was young
Someday, true love would come
If I would just stay in God's plan
And do His every command.

They told me God knows my every need
And someday He would bless me
And the whole world will see
That true love has come
In spite of the storm.

True love has come
True love has come
Two hearts now beat as one
Because true love has come.

*W*hat you just read are lyrics from a song I wrote for my godsister's wedding a few years ago. Wedding singer is just one of the many roles in which I have served in countless wedding ceremonies over the course of my life. I have served as a wedding planner, music director, and ordained minister. I've also had the pleasure of counseling couples before marriage and officiating at their nuptials.

I've been behind the scenes and in front of the scenes in nearly every capacity except for one—being the groom. I have never had the opportunity to look into the eyes of the woman of my dreams and promise to love her for the rest of my life.

In my travels, I have discovered that I am not alone in my quest for love and happiness with that special someone. In fact, I have met countless progressive, accomplished singles who share a similar journey. During candid conversations with singles, many have shared that they often feel unfulfilled, like the "odd person out." These are feelings I can easily understand because I have often felt the same way myself.

As a child, I dreamed of having a good job, a nice house, and a beautiful wife, just like on TV. However, unlike TV, in real life the plot, characters, and happy ending are not all accomplished in thirty minutes—with or without commercials. Life is far more complicated than TV land, yet at the same time, offers far more possibilities.

Fast forward to adulthood. I've been blessed with a great career, which has afforded me the opportunity to live in a nice house, travel to exotic places, and meet some great people. However, the job, the house, the trips—not even the people— have helped me find the right woman to love and marry. It looks like the Beatles were right: "Money can't buy you love."

Being a Christian, I started by praying for answers to my dilemma. As a student of scripture, I understood I had to couple my prayers with some faith and action. So I set out on a quest to find ways to cope with the loneliness that haunted me at night and the frustrations that plagued me by day.

I searched relentlessly until answers started to come. At first I got flippant answers, like, *Stop looking and she will appear; When you least expect it, she will show up,* and; *She might just be standing right in front of you.* Confused, frustrated, and just about to abandon the mission, I figured out why I was getting such meaningless answers. The problem was, I was asking all the wrong questions. So I narrowed my search to one broad question: What am I supposed to do while I look for the right person to marry?

Today, that one question has evolved into the book you are about to read. This book is my clarion call to faith and action for those searching for marital love for the first time, or those hoping to find love again. I pray that as you read this book, you will be inspired to reach for new levels of destiny. In fact, I believe so strongly in the message of this book that I am donating all proceeds to charity.

INTRODUCTION

*A*s a single Christian man, I believe the two most important choices a man can make are the right God and the right girl. The right God offers heaven after earth. The right girl offers heaven on earth. Ladies, the same applies to you (the right God and the right guy).

As for me, I am proud to say that I have found the right God. I hope you have as well. However, finding the woman of my dreams has been complicated—like finding a needle in a haystack. To make matters worse, there was a time in my life when I was bombarded with a lot of discouraging stories about marriage. (Perhaps you can relate.) Over time, however, I discovered something interesting. I discovered these horror stories about the perils of marriage had a common thread: they all came from unhappy people. You know the kind of person who can somehow find a cloud in the sky on the most beautiful sunny day. I concluded these people would probably be unhappy whether single or married.

Moving forward, I decided to intentionally seek out couples that were happily married. As I spent time with these couples,

I made another interesting discovery. I discovered that just as unhappy stories had a common thread, so did happy marriages.

Happy couples had the following in common:

1. They experienced happiness while single.

2. They enjoyed healthy relationships before marriage.

3. They made ongoing efforts to prepare themselves for marriage while single.

In addition to learning from happy couples, I have gained an immeasurable amount of wisdom from well-adjusted singles. However, life itself has proven to be my greatest teacher. The compilation of these life lessons was the beginning of my emancipation from the chains of feeling unloved, unfulfilled, and incomplete as a single. No longer was I going to wallow in the downside of singlehood.

Due to the positive perspectives I gained on dating, marriage, and life in general, I have committed myself to being happy with me before entering into a relationship. Most importantly, I have committed myself to preparing for marriage before committing to marriage. I will share these perspectives, life lessons, and strategies throughout this book.

In the meantime, I have found peace in the belief that it just may be that God is still refining me so I can be at my best for my wife. A related belief is that it just may be that God is still working on my mate because he knows just what I need. Better still, it just may be that God is still working on both of us so we can be our best for each other.

I invite you to join me on a journey designed to help you prepare for marriage. As we take this journey together, I encourage you to go beyond merely dreaming about marriage. Although dreaming is good, in this case, it's not enough. You must start the process of preparing yourself to make your dream a beautiful reality.

In light of everything I have said so far, my purpose for writing this book is to give singles a simple, three-step plan to eventually live out the words, "I Do."

This plan is designed to help you achieve the following:

- Acknowledge the good, the bad, and the ugly from your past.

- Adjust the areas of your life that have been damaged.

- Activate a healthy lifestyle to prepare your heart for marriage.

As you continue reading this book, you will learn to acknowledge, adjust, and activate a healthier lifestyle as a single. This three-step process will provide you with some practical tools to create a more positive you.

If you are ready to join me on this journey of attracting the right man or woman God has just for you, get ready to roll up your sleeves to take on the work of knowing, What to Do Before "I Do."

CHAPTER ONE

THERE'S NOTHING MAGICAL ABOUT THE WORDS, "I DO"

"He who fails to plan, plans to fail."
~Winston Churchill

*M*any couples spend a lot of time and money preparing for a wedding. They will splurge on the wedding dinner, the rehearsal, the reception, and other festivities. (In some cases, brides-to-be become so obsessed with planning the perfect wedding that they morph into overbearing "bridezillas"!) Yet, many of those same couples spend very little time preparing for marital life after the party is over.

There are countless stories of fathers spending excessive amounts of money on weddings that fail in three years or less. However, I have discovered that the root of this problem can be summed up like this:

> TOO MANY COUPLES GIVE IN TO THE PRESSURE OF TRYING TO HAVE THE WEDDING OF THE SEASON INSTEAD OF PREPARING TO HAVE THE MARRIAGE OF A LIFETIME.

An elaborate wedding, a successful wedding dinner, and an over-the-top reception (and all other wedding activities) require time and preparation. Far more time and effort should be put into preparing to enjoy a successful marriage. Yet, year after year, many couples err on the side of focusing on the ceremony and related events.

The Social Root of the Problem

Many people seem to think something transformative takes place when they stand before a wedding officiant and say the words, "I Do." For some reason, many believe saying those two words will somehow wash away all the negativity and pain of their past. Even more amazing, many believe the words, "I Do," can magically erase all the ungodly activities they engaged in at the bachelor or bachelorette party the night before the wedding.

The truth of the matter is there is nothing magical or otherwise about the words, "I Do." They are merely two words unless the people uttering them are willing and prepared to honor them. Consequently, those desirous of a healthy marriage should take pride in being trustworthy people. At the core of every great marriage you will find two trustworthy people.

You've probably heard the expression, "My word is my bond." This old expression has been the ultimate standard of a person's truthfulness. When it comes to wedding vows, honoring them requires a sacred covenant bound by the couple's commitment to truth and loyalty.

Singles that make the best spouses tend to be people who have a track record of accountability. Family members, friends, associates, and others can confirm and attest their integrity. The underlying issue is you cannot expect a person to suddenly be a vow keeper if he or she has no consistent track record. After all, if a person has a habit of breaking promises to loved ones he or she has known all his or her life, the odds of keeping a vow made in a thirty-minute ceremony are very slim.

To sum it all up, honor, trustworthiness, and commitment are the foundation of any successful relationship. Therefore, couples should desire to become living epistles of their vows.

> AS LIVING EPISTLES, COUPLES GIVE LIFE TO THE WORDS, "I DO," INSTEAD OF RELYING ON THE WORDS TO GIVE LIFE TO THEM.

As their love grows, their moral compass is as consistent as time and second nature, like breathing. As a result, these two simple words transform into an earth-shattering mystical love language that has the power to keep vows intact and love alive.

The Spiritual Root of the Problem

So why do so many couples believe two words have the power to sustain their marriage? The answer can be found in scripture. The answer can be traced to Satan's hatred for God's divine plan for his children. In short, the answer can be reduced to two words: SATAN'S COUNTERATTACK.

Starting with the first marriage of Adam and Eve, Satan has been committed to destroying God's plan for marriage and family. In Matthew 16:18 (NKJV), Jesus tells Peter, "On this rock I will build my church, and the gates of Hades shall not prevail against it." While Peter and the other disciples listened to Jesus, Satan listened in as well.

Since God gave this promise specifically to the church (not to the family), the devil knows he will never defeat the church. Therefore, the enemy of our souls has devised a different plan of destruction. His plan is to destroy the institution of marriage and family in order to distract the church from its mission. As a result, most studies conclude that the divorce rate in America has exceeded more than 50 percent.

The Situation: The fact that more than 50 percent of American marriages end in divorce points to one obvious thing: there is no magic in the words, "I Do."

The Solution: Couples must dedicate themselves to preparing to live the words, "I Do," before they say the words on their wedding day.

CHAPTER TWO

DETOXING FROM THE PAST: GETTING THE BAD STUFF OUT SO WE CAN GET THE GOOD STUFF IN

"Detox: A regimen or treatment to remove toxins and impurities from the body."
~Merriam-Webster Dictionary[1]

*J*will never forget the first time I went through a physical detox. This involves abstaining from toxins in order to rid the body of unhealthy substances. For added support and accountability, I decided to join a group under a doctor's care.

Out of all the instructions our doctor gave us, the one that made the most sense to me was this: "Guys, all we're doing is getting the bad stuff out so we can get the good stuff in." Well, this is exactly what I will be covering in this chapter: getting the bad stuff from your past out so you can get the good stuff in that God has for your future. As we go forward, you will start to see what I call "detox scriptures," "detox affirmations," and "detox prayers." I provide these to help you cleanse your mind, body, and soul from anything that may inhibit you from finding love and happiness.

Although the negativity of your past may have caused you pain, over time, that pain can ultimately make you stronger if you grasp this simple twofold lesson. First, you must resolve within yourself what went awry in past experiences. Second, you have to take responsibility for your part in those experiences and corresponding actions that caused you to be in the toxic situation in the first place.

> YOU MUST REMOVE ANY PERSON OR ACTION THAT BRINGS YOU PERSISTENT, TOXIC PAIN. IN ORDER TO BE GOOD TO SOMEONE ELSE, YOU MUST FIRST BE GOOD TO YOURSELF.

Once you understand this principle, you have to take the necessary steps to rid yourself of toxic situations now (and forever).

The late Maya Angelou said, "When you know better, you do better." However, typically, knowing better is not enough. You must take the negative energy from your toxic experiences and use it as fuel to do better.

One example of detoxing from past experiences can be found in the story of training a circus elephant. During the training process, a baby circus elephant is conditioned to be controlled and limited by a chain and a stake. However, if the elephant could break free or detox from the chain and stake, it would be free to be what it was designed to be. Similarly, people can be conditioned to be held captive by various spiritual chains that are formed early in life and through past relationships. Although these bonds may seem unbreakable, they can be broken through the power of God.

Three Pillars for Rebuilding Your Soul/Spirit after a Toxic Relationship

In the very beginning, God created us to enjoy fellowship with him and his people. Before Adam and Eve sinned, God fellowshipped with them in the cool of the day. God also told Adam that it was not good for him to be alone, so he gave him Eve.

From the very beginning, our wise, loving God had a plan to restore broken relationships and broken people. I encourage you to lean on the following three spiritual pillars as you detox from past toxic relationships: prayer, fellowship, and fasting.

1) The Pillar of Prayer

Throughout scripture, countless references attest to the power of prayer. At its most organic core, prayer is the process of finite, flawed people communicating with the only infinite, flawless God. I can assure you that our all-wise God is more concerned about regulating the pulse of his children's hearts than anything else in the universe. Moreover, our Heavenly Father is also concerned about our love lives.

As a child, I remember a deacon in my church who always started his prayers with this phrase: "All wise God, we, your children, come before you as empty vessels before a full fountain." The fountain that old deacon spoke about will never dry up. Even when it comes to broken relationships, Jesus still stands at the door of our hearts waiting for us to invite him in so he can mend our brokenness.

Detox Scripture

"Not that I have already attained, or am already perfected; but I press on, that I may lay hold of that for which Christ Jesus has also laid hold of me. Brethren, I do not count myself to have apprehended; but one thing I do, forgetting those things which are behind and reaching forward to those things which are ahead, I press toward the goal for the prize of the upward call of God in Christ Jesus" (Philippians 3:12-14, NKJV).

Detox Prayer

Dear Lord, I come to you in the mighty name of Jesus, empty and broken. Yet, I believe you can mend the broken pieces of my heart. I believe you can strengthen the weak areas of my emotions. I believe you can help me to love again.

So, Lord, give me the strength to forget the pains of the past. Give me the strength to reach for the blessings you have in store for me. Finally, Lord, give me the strength to press past any and all obstacles in order to forgive myself and the people who caused me so much pain. Amen!

2) The Pillar of Fellowship

In Hebrews 10:25 (NKJV), the apostle Paul instructs Christians to assemble and worship and provides us with an excellent illustration of Christian fellowship. Essentially, we take on being the body of Christ when we uplift each other by serving as God's hands, mouth, and feet to others in this world. In other words, as Christians, we should strive to model our lives after Jesus Christ.

Being part of a strong, Bible-based church fellowship has many benefits. One of the greatest is that we learn how to develop and sustain Bible-based relationships.

Detox Plan for Healthy Relationships

If we relate genuine Christian fellowship to relationship, we see the following principles:

- Love (1 John 3:11 NKJV)
- Honor and devotion (Romans 12:10 NKJV)
- A desire to be good and helpful (Romans 15:14 NKJV)
- A desire to be kind, compassionate, and forgiving (Ephesians 4:32 NKJV)
- A desire to mutually encourage and build each other up (1 Thessalonians 5:11, NKJV)

Detox Prayer for Healthy Relationships

Dear Lord, I come to you in the mighty name of Jesus, seeking your wisdom and guidance as I establish fellowship and relationship with others. First, I thank you for the relationship I have with you as my Lord. Second, I thank you for the relationship I have with the people you placed in my life.

Lord, as I move forward, I pray that through your Word and the Holy Spirit, you will continue to guide me to people and relationships that bring glory to your name and happiness to my heart. Amen!

3) The Pillar of Fasting

Some scars from past relationships can only be overcome through fasting. Even Jesus said in Mark 9:29 (NKJV), "Some situations can only be conquered through prayer and fasting."

Isaiah 58:6 (NKJV) provides us with definitive proof about the emancipating powers of fasting: "Is not this the fast that I have chosen to loose the bands of wickedness, to undo the heavy burdens, and to let the oppressed go free, and that ye break every yoke?" In this passage, Isaiah promises that fasting inspired by God has the ability to literally undo heavy burdens. The literal burden Isaiah is speaking of is a wooden bar that yoked or joined two oxen to each other so they could work as a team and pull a load.

Just as oxen are held captive by yokes, we can also be held captive by the yoke of negative words from toxic relationships that attach themselves to our souls. The beauty of this passage is that fasting inspired by God unties the bands of wickedness that hold yokes of sin in place in our lives. Once the yoke is detached, we no longer have to pull the burdensome load of sin. As a result, we have power over our tongues, our passions, and lifestyles.

Detox Scripture for Fasting

"Is not this the fast that I have chosen to loose the bands of wickedness, to undo the heavy burdens, and to let the oppressed go free, and that ye break every yoke?" (Isaiah 58:6 NKJV).

Detox Prayer

Dear Lord, I come to you in the precious name of Jesus, in need of your power to break the yokes in my life. I believe you have all power in heaven and on earth. So, Lord, as I fast and pray, I will wait in your presence for answers, emotional healing, and future guidance. Amen!

Create Your Spiritual Action Plan

In Matthew 11:29-30 (NKJV), Jesus said, "Take My yoke upon you and learn from Me. For I am gentle and lowly in heart, and you will find rest for your souls. For My yoke *is* easy and My burden is light." Here's a snapshot of a spiritual action plan from a single man I recently counseled.

The Problem
I'm still haunted by the pain of my last relationship.

The Plan
I will not judge my future dating encounters based on my former relationships. I will give each person a chance to be trusted.

The Action Prayer
Jesus, I receive your yoke and release my burdens to YOU!

Now, it's your turn. State your problem and create your action plan. As you go through this exercise, repeat Philippians 4:13 (NKJV) as needed: "I can do all things through Christ who strengthens me."

The Problem

_____

_____

_____

The Plan

_____

_____

_____

The Action Prayer

_____

_____

_____

CHAPTER THREE

ACKNOWLEDGING WHO YOU ARE NOW

"Know thyself."
~Pausanias

*A*t this point, I hope you are starting to see the importance of detoxing. The more you invest in this process, the more you will benefit from it. I applaud you for taking the steps necessary to cleanse yourself from the pains that hinder you from experiencing God's best for your life.

In this and the next few chapters, you will be exposed to the first of three steps for self-improvement. The first step is the process of acknowledging who you are now. With that said, it is time to wholeheartedly commit to continuing the work of spiritually, emotionally, psychologically, and physically detoxing from the lingering pains of your past.

The phrase, "Know thyself" was written on the forecourt of the Temple of Apollo at Delphi. This principle was one of seven concepts that shaped ancient Greek culture and, eventually, our Western mindset.

Socrates said, "What I want to discover at present is the art which devotes its attention to precision, exactness, and the fullest truth." The truth that Socrates desired was first and foremost to discover truth about himself.

What a profound and necessary philosophy. Self-assessment is critical for every dimension of our lives. To be more precise, genuine awareness of where we have been and where we are now is the starting block for every area of personal growth and improvement.

Successful corporations, churches, families, and other institutions often conduct progress reports to assess the past before planning for the future. However, no assessment or progress report is useful unless there is an honest acknowledgement of the facts. As singles, we start developing our healthy lifestyle strategy by acknowledging and accepting the reality of where we are and where we have been.

Assessing where you have been and who you were in past relationships is a great starting point. Our current behavior is significantly shaped by our past experiences. Simply put, we are an emotional, spiritual, physiological, and physical compilation of our past experiences. Past relationships have a significant effect on who we are and who we will eventually become. Self-assessment and periodic reality checks are an extremely important part of growth. In order to experience growth in business and personal relationships, it is important to acknowledge our current situation. Only then can forward progress be made.

How many times have we heard the expression, "I know something is wrong, but I just can't seem to put my finger on the problem"? The fact of the matter is most people are aware when problems exist. However, we often find ourselves stuck because we do not take action. In many cases, we do not take action because we cannot get to the root of the issue.

We must always remember that everyone has negative and positive character traits. Therefore, as the old saying goes, We must strive to "eliminate the negatives, accentuate the positives, and leave the in-betweens alone."

Remember, as we face our flaws we must not become personally discouraged or overly critical of ourselves. Instead, we must understand and accept the reality that everyone has limitations. The process for acknowledgement is as follows:

1. REALIZE there is a problem.

2. REASON with yourself in order to get to the root cause.

3. REPLACE past negative behaviors with new positive behaviors.

Because our society today is bombarded with romantic and sexual images, it is important for singles to begin their quest for satisfaction by sincerely assessing the ways this has affected them. The day-to-day association with explicit romantic and sexual images can have both covert and overt sociological and emotional effects on singles. It is a mathematical and sociological fact that association produces assimilation. Studies show that repeated exposure to and association with a behavior can significantly affect individuals mentally, emotionally, and psychologically.

Music videos, soap operas, commercials, and even some sporting events contain an excessive amount of romantic or sexual exploitation. Even if a person abstains from television, music videos, and other influences, it is virtually impossible to completely escape the negative images of lust that permeate our society.

Though the path to overcoming the negative effects of modern culture will have its share of challenges, victory awaits you if you are willing to stay the course. My pastor used to say, "In order to end the right way, you have to start the right way." In light of my pastor's wisdom, in order to start the process of moving forward the correct way, the first step is to acknowledge where you are now.

How Did I Get Here?

According to many behavioral experts, human behavior is primarily shaped by one's genetics, environment, and experiences. I've designed this chapter to provide you with spiritual and practical tools for getting to the root of negative behaviors that have been shaped by your prism or view of life.

In the remainder of this chapter, I challenge you to identify painful people, places, and events from your past. The goal is to encourage you to face your past and ultimately find freedom. This process is key for moving forward and enjoying a Christ-centered single life in a self-centered society.

A Snapshot of Your Starting Point

"Behold, I was brought forth in iniquity and in sin my mother conceived me" (Psalm 51:5 NKJV). This passage is King David's response to God when he was challenged to get to the root of his sin with Bathsheba. Perhaps your fall from grace is not as dramatic as David's; however, everyone's life has been shaped and driven by genetics, environment, and experiences.

In the space provided below, list three behavioral characteristics you received from your birth parents, your environment, and your experiences.

My Genetics (example: addictive behavior)

1. _____

2. _____

3. _____

My Environment (example: domestic violence in the home)

1. _____

2. _____

3. _____

My Experiences (example: abusive relationship)

1. _____

2. _____

3. _____

A Snapshot of Your Struggles

"Let no one say when he is tempted, 'I am tempted by God;' for God cannot be tempted by evil, nor does He Himself tempt anyone. But each one is tempted when he is drawn away by his own desires and enticed. Then, when desire has conceived, it gives birth to sin; and sin, when it is full-grown, brings forth death" (James 1:13-15 NKJV). This scripture from the book of James explains the root cause and effect of temptation.

Many people make excuses for why they do things that are not right. However, several other factors also play a role in shaping our behavior, such as past traumas that evolve into triggers that define our temptation. In the space provided below, list three people, places, and events that are traumas, triggers, or temptations that have caused pain in your life.

My Traumas (examples: physical, sexual, emotional abuse)

1. _____

2. _____

3. _____

My Triggers (example: music that triggers a painful emotion from the past)

1. _____

2. _____

3. _____

My Temptations (example: a toxic attractive person)

1. _____

2. _____

3. _____

A Snapshot of Your Soul

"Behold, You desire truth in the inward parts, and in the hidden part you will make me to know wisdom" (Psalm 51:6 NKJV). The Greek word for the soul is *psuche*. According to *Thayer and Smith's Bible Dictionary, psuche*[1] can be defined as "the seat of the feelings, desires, and affections." With this in mind, the passage above speaks of God's divine desire for us to come before him with complete transparency. Only when we come clean before God concerning our secret temptations can the healing begin. In the space provided below, list three desires of your will, your heart, and your inner self.

My Will (examples: personal dreams, hopes, and desires)

1. _____

2. _____

3. _____

My Heart (examples: desire for love, affection, and intimacy)

1. _____

2. _____

3. _____

My Inner Self (example: secret desires—good or bad)

1. _____

2. _____

3. _____

CHAPTER FOUR

TOXIC SINGLES—THE ULTIMATE GUIDE

*"There was nothing so right about my negative
relationships; there was something so wrong with me."*
~Hiawatha Hemphill

*I*n order to love unconditionally, we must be free from the
pains brought on by past relationships. In this chapter,
you will be exposed to various toxic personality types you may
have encountered. The goal is to expose you to negative behaviors from your past so that you can make necessary changes for
self-improvement.

As you read through this chapter, be prayerful, consistent,
and most importantly, be honest with yourself and God. Also,
for your convenience, I have provided the following to assist
you on your path toward freedom:

1. Toxic Personality Types

   • As you see yourself in any of the personality types,
     make a commitment to abandon these unhealthy
     behaviors.

- As you identify negative personalities you have dated in the past, make the commitment not to date that kind of person again.

2. Detox Reality Check Section

- This is a fill-in-the-blank section.

- The goal in this section is to document ways you are like or unlike each personality type.

3. Detox Scriptures

- These scriptures are here to give you the spiritual strength you need to break unhealthy relationship patterns.

- Read them and commit to making them a reality in your life.

- Read them silently and aloud.

4. Detox Affirmations

- I provide these affirmations to give you added confidence as you move forward.

- Read them aloud, read them often, and personalize them.

Toxic Personality Types

Ms. Female Hunter

The first toxic personality type is Ms. Female Hunter. This is a woman who has defied the natural order of godly protocol. Traditionally, women have held the belief that men are supposed to be the pursuer. Contrary to this traditional value, instead of allowing men to pursue her, Ms. Female Hunter is the aggressor.

In today's postmodern culture, many women feel that it is perfectly acceptable for women to ask a man out or even chase him down. However, the Bible warns against this type of behavior. One such warning is found in Proverbs, which says, "He who finds a wife finds a good thing, And obtains favor from the Lord" (Proverbs 18:22 NKJV).

In addition to scripture, there is an all-points bulletin from the wise women of the church: "Remember, if you have to run after him to get him, you'll have to run after him to keep him."

Detox Reality Check

How are you most like Ms. Female Hunter?

_____

_____

_____

_____

_____

How are you most *unlike* Ms. Female Hunter?

_____

_____

_____

_____

_____

_____

Detox Scripture

"Wait on the Lord: be of good courage, and he shall strengthen thine heart: wait, I say, on the Lord" (Psalm 27:14 NKJV).

Detox Affirmation

As a woman, I will wait with joy for the one God has prepared for me. In the meantime, I will prepare my mind, body, and soul as I wait for the man God has designed for me.

Mr. Skycap

The concept of Mr. Skycap is taken from skycaps that carry bags for passengers at airports. The downside, however, is the fact that the skycap at the airport never gets the pleasure of enjoying the trip. The skycap only gets a tip sometimes for carrying all those heavy bags.

While the airport skycap carries bags for airline passengers, Mr. Skycap assumes the responsibility of helping women carry and unload their emotional baggage. He carries a woman's bags during the hard times, only to find himself getting a tip of a relationship because she usually boards the plane of life with another man.

Detox Reality Check

How are you most like Mr. Skycap?

_____

_____

_____

_____

_____

_____

How are you most *unlike* Mr. Skycap?

_____

_____

_____

_____

_____

_____

Detox Scripture

"Finally, brethren, whatever things are true, whatever things are noble, whatever things are just, whatever things are pure, whatever things are lovely, whatever things are of good report, if there is any virtue and if there is anything praiseworthy—meditate on these things" (Philippians 4:8 NKJV).

Detox Affirmation

As a man, I will go through the process of changing my spiritual, emotional, and financial habits in order to hear God's voice as he directs me to the one he has prepared for me. As I go through this process, I will not take on the task of carrying the load of unhealthy relationships.

Ms. Fix Him

Ms. Fix Him has a strong desire to use her matriarchal gift to fix men. As a result, she is attracted to men who need to be rescued. She is usually attracted to wounded men she can "mother" (so to speak). This kind of compulsive behavior often leaves her disappointed because she has taken on the impossible task of trying to convert a man into the image of what she believes he should be.

Ms. Fix Him will repeatedly experience unfruitful relationships until she understands she will never be able to create her idea of a perfect man. The thing this woman must be mindful of is she risks the odds of losing herself trying to help a man find himself. Until Ms. Fix Him overcomes the obsessive need to fix someone and starts the process of working on herself, she will remain in this cycle of unhappiness. Most importantly, until she embraces the blessed reality that only Jesus can fix broken lives, she will be perpetually broken.

Detox Reality Check

How are you most like Ms. Fix Him?

_____

_____

_____

_____

_____

_____

How are you most _unlike_ Ms. Fix Him?

_____

_____

_____

_____

_____

Detox Scripture

"Unless the Lord builds the house, they labor in vain who build it; Unless the Lord guards the city, the watchman stays awake in vain" (Psalm 127:1 NKJV).

Detox Affirmation

As a woman, I surrender my desire to fix, create, redesign, mother, and control a man. From this day forward, I vow to stop being a fixer, and I will allow the Holy Spirit to fix me in my broken places.

Mr. or Ms. Goody-Two-Shoes (with a Dangerous Streak)

In life there are "inspector" and "investor" personality types. Inspectors devote themselves to assessing people and situations. Investors devote themselves to finding out what they can do to improve people and situations. Mr. or Ms. Goody-Two-Shoes (with a Dangerous Streak) are normally good-hearted people looking for love in all the wrong places with all the wrong people. As a result, they often find themselves emotionally invested in toxic and even dangerous relationships. Although they may have good hearts, they are bad character inspectors.

This kind of personality flaw can be the result of several factors. Some are attracted to toxic relationships because of an abusive childhood. Others are attracted to toxic relationships because of low self-esteem. Still others find themselves in dangerous relationships because of their unexplainable innate desire to walk on the so-called "wild side."

Reasons for this kind of behavior can run the gamut. It can get complicated, but I'll try to simplify it. At its core, this personality type is unable to tell the difference between love and lust, pleasure and pain, and above all, Mr. Right and Ms. Wrong. The sad commentary is these two have become what I call "numb to love" because they see themselves as worthless and unworthy of healthy, loving relationships.

Detox Reality Check

How are you most like Mr. or Ms. Goody-Two-Shoes
(with a Dangerous Streak)?

_____

_____

_____

_____

_____

_____

How are you most _unlike_ Mr. or Ms. Goody-Two-Shoes
(with a Dangerous Streak)?

_____

_____

_____

_____

_____

_____

Detox Scripture

"Do not be unequally yoked together with unbelievers.
For what fellowship has righteousness with lawlessness?
And what communion has light with darkness?" (2
Corinthians 6:14 NKJV).

Detox Affirmation

I commit to allowing God to deliver me from unhealthy desires that cause me to engage in relationships with people who are not good for me.

Mr. or Ms. Loop

The Mr. and Ms. Loop personality type is similar to the repeat or loop option found on many electronic devices, which provide the option of hearing a favorite sequence of music over and over. Having the ability to hear a song over and over can be quite a luxury. In contrast, imagine a listener making a mistake and looping a song that is not a favorite, or that he or she finds irritating—very unpleasant to the ear. In that case, the song provides no real listening pleasure.

Now, imagine countless men and women who have somehow gotten stuck in the negative relationship loop. Until they break free and change their theme song, they will experience the same kind of person and same kind of negative experience over and over again.

Detox Reality Check

How are you most like Mr. and Ms. Loop?

_____

_____

_____

_____

_____

How are you most *unlike* Mr. and Ms. Loop?

_____

_____

_____

_____

_____

_____

Detox Scripture

"Test all things; hold fast what is good. Abstain from every form of evil" (1 Thessalonians 5:21-22 NKJV).

Detox Affirmation

I commit to allowing God to break the spiritual and emotional strongholds of my past that have caused me to repeatedly engage in toxic relationships.

Mr. or Ms. Mini Me

Mr. and Ms. Mini Me are very interesting personalities. They typically view themselves as worthless or small, so they often negatively esteem themselves as below others. In fact, they seem to get some form of validation by affirming others while demeaning themselves—a classic personality problem.

Recall the story of the twelve spies Moses sent to scout out the Promised Land. Only Joshua and Caleb were optimistic, confident, and self-assured enough to believe they could overcome the giants that stood between them and their blessings.

Mr. and Ms. Mini Me would have been numbered among the other ten. And as such, they will miss out on many great relationships and, ultimately, their soul mates as long as they see others as unapproachable and above them.

Detox Reality Check

How are you most like Mr. or Ms. Mini Me?

_____

_____

_____

_____

_____

_____

How are you most *unlike* Mr. or Ms. Mini Me?

_____

_____

_____

_____

_____

_____

Detox Scripture

"For God has not given us a spirit of fear, but of power and of love and of a sound mind" (2 Timothy 1:7 NKJV).

Detox Affirmation

I commit to learning to see myself daily as God sees me. Since God sees me as more than a conqueror, I will stop trying to live up to anybody else's lower expectations. I will allow Christ to live through me.

Ms. Ticktock

Ms. Ticktock is a woman who hears the proverbial biological clock ticking loudly! She is discouraged because she does not have a mate or children, and her time seems to be running out.

Ladies in this category need to be encouraged that modern medical technology and adoption provide hope and inspiration. Moreover, these women need to grasp hold to the truth that we are not controlled by "the sun of God" time, but by the Son of God's time! It's not over until God says so. Just ask Abraham and Sarah!

Detox Reality Check

How are you most like Ms. Ticktock?

_____

_____

_____

_____

_____

_____

How are you most *unlike* Ms. Ticktock?

_____

_____

_____

_____

_____

_____

Detox Scripture

"Wait on the Lord; be of good courage, and He shall strengthen your heart; wait, I say, on the Lord!" (Psalm 27:14 NKJV).

Detox Affirmation

I commit to laying my fears of time at the feet of the God who created and controls time and space. I trust my Father God to send the son or daughter he has designed for me.

Mr. Player

Mr. Player plays games with a woman's heart in order to satisfy his overinflated ego. There are various categories of Mr. Player. There are corporate, ghetto fabulous, and even ecclesiastical males who fit into these categories.

This kind of man is unwilling to commit nor give anything of substance to a relationship. He tends to be arrogant, selfish, and narcissistic. As a result, he will often hold women hostage to his self-serving agenda. This is particularly dangerous because true love gives life; it does not take hostages! I remind you, Mr. Player, the boomerang usually returns on the same path—and to the one who threw it.

Detox Reality Check

How are you most like Mr. Player?

_____

_____

_____

_____

_____

How are you most *unlike* Mr. Player?

_____

_____

_____

_____

_____

Detox Scripture

"Do not be deceived, God is not mocked; for whatever a man sows, that he will also reap" (Galatians 6:7 NKJV).

Detox Affirmation

I commit to cleansing myself from behaviors that cause me to hurt, manipulate, and objectify women. I lay my selfishness, pride, and arrogance at the altar of repentance so that I can love with a pure heart.

Mr. or Ms. Drama

Among the seven billion plus people on the planet, there are those who are a part of problems . . . and those who are part of solutions. Well, Mr. and Ms. Drama are the king and queen of problems. If things are peaceful, they will find a way to cause chaos and sustain negative energy. Their words and deeds usually cause social, emotional, or psychological problems for themselves and others.

Their flair for the dramatic can cause even the calmest situations to devolve into their own negative episode, movie of the week, miniseries, epic drama, or sequel. This personality type has mastered the art of playing the role of a victim, when in reality he or she is the villain. While words have the power to give life to the hearer, their words are like verbal daggers that cut with a deadly thrust.

Detox Reality Check

How are you most like Mr. and Ms. Drama?

_____

_____

_____

_____

How are you most *unlike* Mr. and Ms. Drama?

Detox Scripture

"Finally, brethren, whatever things are true, whatever things are noble, whatever things are just, whatever things are pure, whatever things are lovely, whatever things are of good report, if there is any virtue and if there is anything praiseworthy—meditate on these things" (Philippians 4:8 NKJV).

Detox Affirmation

I commit to learning a new way of thinking in order to form new patterns of positive behavior. Also, I repent and denounce any harmful words or actions that have brought pain to others.

Mr. or Ms. I Can Never Be Alone

Mr. and Ms. I Can Never Be Alone have a personality that constantly needs to be involved in some kind of relationship. I like to refer to these two individuals as "relationship opportunists." Because of their unquenchable thirst for attention, they tend to jump at any opportunity to be in a relationship.

People with this personality type often have many unresolved issues from past relationships because they never allow time for healing between relationships. As a result, they carry unresolved issues into new relationships.

One of my good friends became involved with a classic version of Ms. I Can Never Be Alone. He had been seeing this young lady for about three months, and the relationship seemed to be progressing despite a few minor differences. One day, this woman asked my friend to come over to her house because she needed to talk to him. Once inside the house, she immediately broke up with him. Shocked and bewildered, my friend encountered the surprise of meeting his replacement on the front steps as he was leaving!

Detox Reality Check

How are you most like Mr. or Ms. I Can Never Be Alone?

_____

_____

_____

_____

_____

How are you most *unlike* Mr. or Ms. I Can Never Be Alone?

_____

_____

_____

_____

_____

_____

Detox Scripture

"I will lift up my eyes to the hills—from whence comes my help? My help comes from the Lord who made heaven and earth" (Psalm 121:1-2 NKJV).

Detox Affirmation

I commit to learning to depend on God for my contentment rather than relying on a relationship to validate me.

Detoxing and Moving Forward

Congratulations on doing something many people will never do. You have just taken a hard look at who you are and who you have been. You should be proud of yourself for committing to doing the work. That, my friend, takes courage and humility to admit your flaws.

You are moving forward on the path toward healing and wholeness. Remember, sometimes when you go through a body detox you feel worse before you feel better. The same may be true in this process. Don't get discouraged if you don't see immediate results or changes. As you may know, any kind of detox takes time. After all, behavioral flaws learned from past relationships did not develop overnight either. Be patient.

Now that you have done the hard work, it's time to go on to the next step of adjusting your life plan for the new you. As you go through this process, I encourage you to make the detox scriptures and affirmations a daily part of your life. Don't be surprised if God opens your mind to more healing scriptures as you go along. Also, don't be surprised if you feel compelled to personalize or add to the detox affirmations I provided for you. In fact, I strongly encourage you to do just that. So, embrace this new opportunity! Personalize it! Own it! Fight for it! It's your life and your destiny!

One last instruction before we go to the next step: be open to the secret things that the Holy Spirit will reveal to you about you as you go forward. If you are ready, it's time to make some adjustments in order to be a better you.

CHAPTER FIVE

ACKNOWLEDGING WHO I WANT TO BE

There is a poem entitled *That's Not My Job* [1] that always gets me pumped up for a new challenge. The poem tells the story of an important job that needed to be done. Four people were assigned to it: Everybody, Somebody, Anybody, and Nobody. As the group approached the job, Everybody was confident that Somebody would step up to the plate. Interestingly, it was a job that Anybody could have done, yet Nobody did. Then, Somebody got angry because it was Everybody's responsibility. However, Everybody thought Anybody could do the job, but Nobody realized Everybody was not going to take action. At the end of the day, Everybody ended up blaming Somebody since Nobody did a job Anybody could have done.

In your life as a single person open for love, you have the option to be like the characters in this story and do nothing, or you can take action. You have the exciting opportunity to start the process of adjusting your life in order to enjoy the best God has for you.

I once played on a basketball team. I remember a certain game when my team was down by twenty points at the halftime break. As we approached the locker room, we braced ourselves to be scolded by our coach. However, to our surprise, our coach did the exact opposite. Instead of scolding us, he told us how much he believed in us. Then he proceeded to give us a come-back game plan based on this theme: "We are going to win by making the right adjustments."

In the second half we implemented our coach's strategy and ultimately won the game. Just as my coach believed in our team, I believe in you. I believe you can be victorious as a single if you are willing to commit to making needed adjustments in your life.

Now that you have acknowledged and accepted the realty of being single, it's time to adjust your life plan. If you are ready, let's take it to the next level.

One of the most significant steps to adjusting your game plan is to start the process of living completely in the now. Men and women should start the process of adjusting to living a life of completeness, wholeness, and happiness TODAY.

If this concept could be bottled up, the warning label would simply read as follows:

> "WARNING: PLACING YOUR LIFE, DREAMS, AND ASPIRATIONS ON HOLD WHILE WAITING FOR MR. OR MRS. RIGHT CAN HAVE SEVERE SIDE EFFECTS."

Many people buy into the false notion that the race toward happiness, success, and fulfillment can only commence at the sound of wedding bells. When we buy into this mythical belief system, we block our journey to happiness. As you consider this revelation, read the following affirmation aloud.

AFFIRMATION

From this day forward, I will live my life with purpose, passion, and persistence. I will not wait for tomorrow; I resolve to make the necessary adjustments now in the following areas:

- Spiritual Development
- Personal Development
- Career and Professional Advancement
- Financial Empowerment and Fiscal Responsibility

Use the space below to add additional areas in which you are not currently living in the moment. Be honest with yourself and be creative as you resolve to make improvements in these categories.

I resolve to make the necessary adjustments NOW in the following additional areas:

1. _____

2. _____

3. _____

4. _____

5. _____

6. _____

At its core, the process of adjustment involves making alterations to help something fit or become more functional. A good tailor alters the length of a garment during a final fitting. A winning coach changes the game strategy at halftime. A progressive corporation changes product lines in order to keep pace with the competition. The tailor, the coach, and the corporation will only achieve their desired outcomes when they consciously make these changes or adjustments. In order for single people to live happily, they must commit to making conscious lifestyle adjustments that cause them to live in the present, productively.

One of the strongest ways to fortify the process of creating a conscious lifestyle adjustment begins by controlling yourself. Self-control is the key internal virtue needed to accomplish personal victories. The best way to practice self-control is to start by controlling the voices within.

Perhaps you are familiar with the classic image of a person making an important life decision with an angel on one shoulder and a demon on the other. Like it or not, many of our life decisions are based on making choices with both good and bad influences in mind. Our attunement to making the best decisions for our lives is directly correlated to how clearly we can hear the voices within our souls.

Many psychologists use the analogy of listening to the voices within. I can already hear you asking, "What are these voices within? How do I control them?" Remember, only you can answer this question, so let's get started with the process.

Embarking on Your Verbal Detox

"Positive words unleash creative forces, but negative words unleash destructive forces."
~Hiawatha Hemphill

From my past relationships, I have learned very powerful lessons about myself and how I relate to women. I discovered that good relationships left me with blessings that continued to ripple in my life for years to come. As I matured, I began to see that even my toxic relationships gave me invaluable lessons for my future dating experiences. And the great relationships gifted me with both blessings and lessons.

As you prepare to cleanse yourself from negative words from past relationships and move forward into a healthier dating life, it is important for you to understand and embrace the process below.

GOOD RELATIONSHIPS, even when they have ended, leave us with the blessing of experiencing our worth and the worth of another person. The key to moving forward is to accept, and most importantly, appreciate the blessings of these relationships.

NEGATIVE RELATIONSHIPS are often rooted in negative words that, over time, have morphed into negative actions. These relationships can teach us lessons on how to set healthy boundaries for future relationships.

When GREAT RELATIONSHIPS end, they leave us with the following gifts:

- The blessing of sharing our lives with a special person

- Lessons that further sharpen us for that one person designed for each of us

- The blessing and the lesson of developing a healthy, platonic friendship

By embracing these three truths, you begin the detox process with a positive attitude. Now you are prepared to get ready for a better you.

Overcoming Negative Words

The first step to becoming healthy as a single person is to cleanse yourself from negative words that have been spoken over your life. This cleansing process is necessary as you embark on your path to creating richer dating experiences. Words can be debilitating and destructive. They can delay you from reaching your destiny if you allow them to take up residence in your mind.

There is a very small South African animal that has the ability to conquer and subdue animals twice its size. The secret to this animal's power is that it has the unique ability to methodically take small pieces out of a larger animal as it completes its conquest.

The smaller animal continues this process until the larger animal becomes weak and defenseless. At that point, the smaller animal swoops in for the kill. This slow, methodical weakening is exactly what negative words can do to your spirit. Toxic words take small pieces out of our spirits, wear us down, and leave us vulnerable and defenseless.

The twenty negative statements on the following page can both knowingly and unknowingly inflict pain upon you. As you read them, distinguish which ones resonate with you the most and determine how you can begin to start to cleanse the most damaging ones from your spirit.

TOP TWENTY BEEN THERE, DONE THAT, AND HEARD IT ALL BEFORE LIST FOR SINGLES

1. You mean to tell me you're not married YET?
2. What are you waiting on?
3. You know . . . you're getting older!
4. You know the older you get, the harder it is to have children.
5. You're just too picky.
6. I don't think you really want to get married. Do you?
7. What are you looking for?
8. You must be looking for someone perfect!
9. You know God may not give you what you want; he may just give you what you need.
10. Are you gay or bisexual?
11. You must be a player.
12. You must be a gold digger.
13. I have someone I want you to meet. Now he (or she) is not the nicest looking person, but he (or she) is really spiritual.
14. Are you a eunuch?
15. You'll probably never get married because you're too set in your ways.
16. You know it's better to marry than burn.
17. I don't think you know what you want.
18. Looks are not everything, you know.
19. Stop looking! That's when you'll find your mate!
20. Stop running behind a man! Let him find you.

Cleansing Oath for Singles

Now that you've read the top twenty list, I know you are pretty fired up. It's time to take the Cleansing Oath for Singles.

STEP ONE: Denounce and Declare

From this day forth, I will purify myself of any negative statements that take me away from my destiny. I will no longer allow negative words or toxic people to affect me spiritually, mentally, or emotionally.

STEP TWO: Take Your Spiritual Vitamin

I will fortify my spirit through the power of scripture, prayer, and fasting.

STEP THREE: Pray

I will pray for any person who sends negative words and energy into my life.

As you work through this step, remember the words of the Christian theologian and author, Lewis B. Smedes:[2] "To forgive is to set a prisoner free and discover that the prisoner was you."

STEP FOUR: Guard Your Heart

I will develop strategies for guarding myself against people with reckless tongues. I make a choice today and every day not to entertain negative thoughts about my single life ever again. Proverbs 18:21 (NKJV) declares, "Death and life are in the power of the tongue, and those who love it will eat its fruit."

STEP FIVE: Renounce and Rebuild

As I remove negative words from my life, I will strike out every statement that stops me from living my single life to the fullest.

The "New You" Challenge

As you move forward, remember the short but powerful poem entitled *That's Not My Job*. As a refresher, there was an important job that needed to be done. As a result, four people—Everybody, Somebody, Anybody, and Nobody—were all faced with a challenge but did nothing.

As a single person who is open for love, you have the option to be like the characters in this story and do nothing. Or you can take action and keep making adjustments to reach your goals.

CHAPTER SIX

THE STORY OF THE INVISIBLE GIRL

"Relationships can be complicated,
but love is simple and pure."
~Hiawatha Hemphill

*O*ver the years, *The Brady Bunch* show kept fans tuning in every week to see what was going to happen next. The story you are about to read is somewhat different, yet like every episode in *The Brady Bunch* series, there is a happy ending. To this day, there are times when I catch myself singing *The Brady Bunch* theme song.

Like Carol Brady, the young woman in this story is a lovely lady. However, unlike Carol, she starts with no daughters and no sons. To make matters worse, the lady in this story starts with no prospects of a fellow to marry, her life plan seems derailed, and her hope chest seems to be simply an afterthought. Perhaps you know someone in this situation (or can relate to this on a personal level).

The classic question singles have asked for generations is this: Does true love exist? My answer is a resounding, "Yes!"

God is the essence of true love and being that we are created in his image, we cannot help but exude that love to others.

I know we've all heard the phrase, "Nobody is perfect." This is true. However, this should not stop you from believing you can have someone who is perfect for YOU.

> THERE IS SOMEONE IN THE WORLD RIGHT NOW HOPING AND PRAYING TODAY THAT YOU WILL CROSS HIS OR HER PATH.

One of the biggest challenges single women face is complying with Proverbs 18:22, which speaks about the man finding the woman. I have had many conversations with women who have expressed their respectful frustration concerning this spiritual truth. For women who are proactive "go getters" by nature, I can only imagine how tough this must be. It is my prayer that I can provide single ladies with a new perspective on waiting for their Ephesians 5 husband.

The Story of the Invisible Girl

What you are about to read is a story of how God honored a dear friend of mine because she stayed true to his Word. As you read through this chapter, you will experience her struggles while waiting on God, her insecurities about herself, and ultimately her reward for waiting for the man to find her.

Many Americans have either read the book or seen the movie *The Invisible Man*. The plot is quite intriguing. It chronicles the life of a man living an underground lifestyle that causes him to become invisible to mainstream society. The story I am about to tell you is just as fascinating as the invisible man. This storyline may be even more intriguing because it is about a beautiful woman longing for romantic love.

How I Met "Ms. Invisible"

During my first year of graduate school, I met a very attractive young lady. For the sake of her privacy, we will call her Ms. Invisible. She was five feet nine inches tall, with an athletic body. Her hair was long, and her eyes were a hypnotic hazel color. She was the kind of woman you might see on the cover of a fashion magazine. Ms. Invisible was easily a "10" in my book. But for some reason, she was always by herself. Even at the school's social gatherings, she never had a date or even a girlfriend tagging along.

At first, I attributed her singleness to the fact that she had a full-time job and carried a full course load in one of the top graduate programs in the country. In addition to being simply gorgeous, she was extremely intelligent. As we entered our second semester, Ms. Invisible and I started to develop a friendship. Since she was the only female, and I was the only student of color in our classes, we often found ourselves studying together. As our friendship started to blossom, I began to wonder, *How could this gorgeous woman still be on the market? Why is this beautiful, intelligent, progressive, professional woman still single?*

Although Ms. Invisible was extremely attractive, I never made a move because I was still healing from a previous relationship. As a result, our relationship quickly developed into a very close platonic friendship. This was the first time I'd had a drop-dead gorgeous woman as a close friend. Over time, this would prove to be the best thing for both of us.

As our friendship deepened, she slowly started to confide in me. I was becoming a big brother to her. After our evening classes, I would walk her to her car. This was our time to unwind and catch up on each other's lives outside the classroom. To my surprise, during one of those dark walks she started asking me some deep, introspective questions about herself. The main question she continually asked was, "Do you think I'm pretty?"

Given her appearance, that question was a no-brainer for me. I would always say, "Girl, I think you are beautiful inside and out." Her response was always the same. "You're just saying that because you're my buddy." I'd quickly respond by saying something like, "Girl, you need to take some of that money you're making at that big firm and buy yourself a mirror. You are gorgeous!" She would typically return my compliment with a nervous laugh. Then she would again follow up by saying, "I'm serious. Do you really think I am pretty? Or are you just trying to make me feel better?"

Since I had just completed a basic psychology course, I started thinking there was something deeper going on with her. Why was this beautiful woman persistently asking me this same question? Why couldn't she see her own beauty? This girl was one of the most beautiful women on campus, yet none of the guys seemed to even notice her. I couldn't understand why they couldn't see what I saw. At that point, I was convinced something had to be going on below the surface.

True Friendship in Action

Our relationship progressed to the point where we could talk to each other about anything. I started asking her, "What's really going on with you? Why are you doubting yourself and your beauty?" With tears filling her big, beautiful, hazel eyes, she said, "If I am so pretty, then why haven't any of the guys asked me for a date?" Then, in a more agitated tone she asked, "And why am I still single?"

At that point, I was completely at a loss for words. In the past, I had always been able to go to my so-called encouragement well. But that time, I had no solid answers for her. I had no comeback, no philosophical maybes, and no humor to sidetrack her pain.

I had never seen her like this. It was clear to me that my usual comebacks were not going to be strong enough to quench her growing emotional fire. I had to act fast.

As the conversation accelerated, I started to feel my friend's pain. Ms. Invisible started unveiling some of her deepest and most painful feelings to me. Her doubts and fears seemed to intensify with each passing moment. Desperation started to make a home in her mind. She couldn't understand why she seemed frozen in a hopeless state—especially when I constantly told her she was going to make some man very happy someday.

Questions and Answers

Over time, I started to see the situation from her perspective. Suddenly, her questions and feelings began making perfect sense to me. I could see her fears were motivated by rock-hard "facts." She was what men back in the day would call a "perfect 10." It must have been devastating for her to be such a looker while feeling so invisible.

Realizing the severity of the situation, I became more determined than ever to help Ms. Invisible become visible. I was committed to finding a way for her to be visible to herself and everyone else. If I played the "humor card" I would have been insensitive. Playing the old "It's going to be okay card," would have been useless. In fact, every combination of encouragement I had used in the past would have been unfruitful at that stage of the game. Something sure and dependable was needed for this situation. I reached deep within myself and pulled out the only sure card I could play—trust in God!

I told her, "I don't have all the answers, but I know God has a plan for your life." I paused as I could see her wheels turning. Then I told her, "I truly believe one day God is going to send someone special into your life." These words of faith seemed to pacify her for the moment because her big, infectious smile returned. As she drove away, I felt a sense of relief because she seemed okay for now. I saw my friend feel good for the first time in a long time. I was glad I could give her some sense of hope in what seemed to her to be a hopeless situation. I can still remember my joy in helping her feel good.

The Man Who Saw Her

Over the next few months, our academic load got heavier, and we didn't have much time for our special brother-sister conversations. Even though our schedules didn't allow us to spend as much time together, our friendship remained as solid as ever. Occasionally, she would still ask me if I thought she was pretty. Over time, I realized that my affirmation seemed to be all she needed. I was unaware at the time that Ms. Invisible was teaching me a valuable life lesson. She showed me that women need and deserve to have men in their lives who are willing to tell them that they are beautiful inside and out.

One day after class, she ran toward me with the biggest smile on her face. She started yelling, "I met someone, and I want you to meet him." She wanted to get my big brother stamp of approval. She was so excited about this new guy. In fact, she was so excited that before the end of the week, I met him. Upon meeting him, I immediately gave him the big brother examination. Based on his honesty, humility, and most importantly, his lack of "game," I must say I was thoroughly impressed. He passed with flying colors.

Ms. Invisible had finally connected with a man who could see her. She found a man who could see how beautiful she was, and was making plans to keep her for life. She was overwhelmed with excitement about her new love. My excitement for her seemed to take her exhilaration over the top. Her enthusiasm about my approval was another valuable lesson I learned about women.

> IT BECAME CRYSTAL CLEAR TO ME THAT WOMEN NEED AND DESIRE TO HEAR THEIR FATHERS, BROTHERS, OR SOME MAN WHO IS SPECIAL TO THEM AFFIRM THEIR CHOICES IN LOVE MATTERS.

One day during class, she passed me a note that said she had something to tell me after class. I knew her relationship was moving pretty fast because she had given me a play-by-play account of how things were going. Still, I wondered what she needed to speak to me about. After class, she rushed over to me with her hands in her pockets. I can still remember her having the biggest smile on her face as she said, "I have something to show you." Before I knew it, she was flashing one of the most beautiful engagement rings I had ever seen.

We celebrated her joy right there in the middle of the classroom. Normally, she was very polished and reserved. But in the exhilaration of the moment, she did not care what anybody thought about our spontaneous celebration. After a few minutes that felt like a few hours, our celebration came to a close. She thanked me with a big smile and happily walked out the door to meet her new fiancé.

After she left the room, some of the guys in the class immediately approached me. They finally saw her. Suddenly, they wanted to know about the pretty girl who had just left the room. One of the guys just cut to the chase with a litany of questions: "Who was that? Where did she come from? Can you hook me up with her?"

I responded with the following series of answers: "First of all, she has been in our classes for the last two years. Second, as for hooking you up, that's now off the table. She just got engaged this morning."

Lessons from Ms. Invisible

What's the takeaway from this story? Why were these guys suddenly so interested in a girl who had been in classes with them for two years? Perhaps the more interesting question is:

"Why had they not noticed her until the day she was officially off the dating market?" After years of replaying this story over and over in my head, I believe there are several lessons to be learned here.

Lesson One: Understand God's Protection vs. God's Punishment

God always has a plan for our lives. His plan is always infinitely greater than our finite minds can comprehend. Since God knows all things, giving us what's best for our lives is easy for him. It is God's pleasure to give good gifts to his children. As in the case of Ms. Invisible, God had set a plan in motion of which she was oblivious. She desperately yearned for love. And God was constantly at work in the background. Even in her hours of frustration and despair, God had my friend's heart in mind all along.

Unknown to us at the time, God had divinely caused this beautiful woman to become virtually invisible. Perhaps one day in heaven she will tell me how she really felt during those days. I can only imagine the battles that raged in the secret chambers of her mind.

In the years that followed, I met a number of single women who felt invisible. This seems to be a prevailing phenomenon in today's society.

I encourage you not to panic. Even when it seems you are invisible to men all around you, there is hope! At the peak of Ms. Invisible's storm, she must have felt as if God were punishing her. Unbeknownst to her, God was doing something far greater and more loving. He was protecting her.

God's arms of protection had kept her from all the potentially painful, broken relationships she may have encountered with the wrong men. God's way of protecting her was to hide her from every other man except the two men who needed to see her in that season.

IF YOU FEEL YOU ARE INVISIBLE, REMEMBER, GOD IS NOT PUNISHING YOU. HE JUST MIGHT BE DIVINELY HIDING YOU FOR THE ONE HE HAS DESIGNED JUST FOR YOU.

Lesson Two: There's a Time to Be Pursued and a Time to Be Preserved

For most single men, the pursuit of a beautiful woman can be exciting. But the case of Ms. Invisible left them asking, "Why did God allow me to see her as a sister and friend?" and, "Why did he allow me to see her, but not allow me to pursue her for myself?" For almost two years, I had held fast to my commitment to protect and honor the special friend God had placed in my care. I had faithfully kept her purity in sacred trust as if she were my blood sister.

After many years of soul-searching, I finally found the answer. God allowed me to see her because, as her Christian brother and friend, he entrusted to me the preservation of her heart.

This experience caused me to see women and my dating life from a whole new perspective. I no longer saw women as objects to be chased and conquered. I then understood that as a Christian man, I was charged with a far greater responsibility. God does not always want us to pursue women. Sometimes, God plants women in our lives so we can preserve them for another man. In these cases, God places them in our lives to be our friends, sisters, and fellow travelers along the road of life.

I have discovered that God did not create women just to feed men's carnal needs to hunt, conquer, and place trophies on our proverbial male mantelpiece. My assignment for Ms. Invisible was to protect her until the right man could see her. I was assigned to keep watch over her and preserve her until the right man would preserve her for life.

Lesson Three: God Has Men Who Can Only Have Eyes for You

The moment I met Ms. Invisible's new boyfriend, I could tell he had not dated many women. He was shy and had no charismatic swagger. However, in the fullness of time, God gave this man the ability to see my friend. In the words of the songwriter, "He only had eyes for her." In the past, she had felt the pains of invisibility. But after they met, his sights locked in on her.

That shy, unassuming man courted my beautiful friend with unrelenting zeal. He saw her, pursued her, and ultimately desired to marry her. The man God had created just for her had found her. She was realizing her hopes and dreams. She was experiencing the unfailing love of God, and the unconditional love of a godly man. God blessed her with a man who saw her in a way no other man ever could.

If you feel invisible, I pray this story will renew, restore, and redirect you back to the beauty that lies within you. My hope is that you will learn to rest in that secret place God has prepared especially for you.

Today, my friend is no longer invisible. She has a husband and children who love, cherish, and see her. Rest on the promises of God, knowing that even when you feel invisible, someone will eventually see you. It happened to my friend Ms. Invisible. It can happen to you, too.

The Role of a Godly Wife:
The Nuts and Bolts of Saying "I Do" For Women

As I shared with you before (and will repeat again), the words "I Do" have no transformative or magical power. Single women must start the process of preparing for "I Do" while they are waiting for marriage. Ephesians 5:22 (NKJV) says, "Wives, submit to your own husbands, as to the Lord."

Because the words "I Do" have no supernatural means of causing women to submit to their husbands, they must start the process of submission long before they get married. Under normal circumstances, this process starts early in life when a young girl learns to submit to her parents and other trusted authority figures.

Proverbs 31:10 (NKJV) asks the question, "Who can find a virtuous woman?" The passage goes on to describe her as follows: "The heart of her husband doth safely trust in her, so that he shall have no need of spoil. She will do him good and not evil all the days of her life." Just the thought that there is a person in the world who can be trusted forever is a priceless promise. The thought that God designed women with a special ability to keep the secrets of a man's heart for the rest of his life is a gift of unlimited value.

According to Bible scholars, Proverbs 31 is a lesson of wisdom taught to King Lemuel by his mother. King Lemuel's mother encouraged him to look for a woman of faith who would be committed to him as a marriage partner and mother to their future children. As you read through Proverbs 31, you find that King Lemuel's mother was quite thorough in her description of the wife he should look for. This wise mother advised him to look for a woman who was a time conscious, caring homemaker, with inner and outer beauty that can only come from a holy lifestyle.

After studying the Proverbs 31 model of womanhood, I have condensed the role of an exceptional woman into the following primary characteristics: helper, hoverer, and healer.

The Helper

The first characteristic of an exceptional woman is to be a helper. Genesis 2:18 (NKJV) reads, "And the Lord God said, 'It is not good that man should be alone; I will make him a helper comparable to him.'" In this scripture, God is crystal clear about the importance of male-female relationships. We can also clearly see from this passage that God's first intention for Eve was to be a helpmeet to Adam.

Interestingly, the word "helper or helpmeet" is one of the most frequently misunderstood terms in the Bible. In their original Hebrew form, the two words "help" and "meet" are derived from the words "ezer" and "k'enegdo." "Ezer" means "to rescue, to save, to be strong."

The miracle of childbirth is the one and only gateway into life. As a result, women are like saviors to men because they give them life. The birth process is often described as going through the valley of the shadow of death. A strong, loving mother makes the decision to go through this valley of pain in order to save her child from death.

The Hoverer

The second characteristic of an exceptional woman is to be a hoverer. According to Titus 2:4 (NKJV), "A wife should love her husband and her children." Deuteronomy 32:11 (NKJV) speaks of a good woman being "like an eagle that stirs up its nest and hovers over its young, that spreads its wings to catch them and carries them aloft."

Proverbs 31 describes the woman as an individual dedicated to serving or hovering over her husband and children. She hovers over her family tirelessly with unselfish devotion. Her industrious nature is not just confined to her family; it is known throughout her community. She is often the topic of positive discussion at the city's main gathering places.

The Healer

The third characteristic of an exceptional woman is her unique ability to bring healing to her family and community. Proverbs 31:10-12 (NKJV) reads: "Who can find a virtuous wife? For her worth is far above rubies. The heart of her husband safely trusts her; so he will have no lack of gain. She does him good and not evil all the days of her life." A woman who gives her husband the option to put his heart in her hands is the ultimate expression of love. In addition, she gives her husband the sacred gift of perpetual healing.

The Story of the Invisible Girl
Summing It All Up

If you are a woman who at least sometimes feels invisible, I want you to understand several things. First, I want you to know that your Heavenly Father sees you. Not only does he see you, he loves you. In fact, he proved his love by creating you with your own special uniqueness and beauty.

Second, God wants you to see yourself the way he sees you. He wants you to see your uniqueness and beauty. The ability to see and appreciate the beauty that lives within you is your God-given right, so embrace it. Embrace the reality that there has never been—nor ever will be—another you.

Third, you were born to be seen by others, and ultimately by a man who will love you. Just as my friend Ms. Invisible was created to be seen by the man God had for her, you were created to be seen by the man he has designed for you.

This phenomenal act of God's love is demonstrated in the first marriage between Adam and Eve, which is recorded in Genesis 2. In this narrative, God put Adam to sleep and took one of the ribs from his body in order to create Eve.

Imagine what would have happened if Adam's rib had gotten discouraged and gotten out of place. Adam's rib was in place and ready when God was ready for it. Like Adam's rib, you must be in place and ready when God is ready for you.

PERHAPS YOU FEEL INVISIBLE BECAUSE YOUR ADAM IS ASLEEP. IT MAY BE THAT YOUR ADAM IS UNDER GOD'S RECONSTRUCTION PLAN, BEING PREPARED JUST FOR YOU.

In your meantime, it is my prayer for you that you will remain in place until God supernaturally redesigns you to be the helper, hoverer, and healer for your Adam.

CHAPTER SEVEN

THE PARABLE OF THE DIAMOND IN THE SAND

*I*n the last chapter, we explored one of the greatest challenges for a single woman—obeying God's will and waiting for the right man to find her. However, the quest to find "the one" is equally challenging for men. Statements such as, "When you stop looking, that's when love will appear," seem to contradict the command of Proverbs 18:22. How can a single man stop looking when the Bible speaks of a man finding a wife? My goal in this chapter is to provide single men with a new perspective on finding their "good thing." Note that I said men must *find* their good thing. In order to find something, you must search for it.

What you are about to read is a parable the Lord gave me during one of my lowest periods as a single man. As you read this parable, notice the importance of allowing God to lead you as you search for a mate. When you allow God to lead you, your search will be fruitful no matter how overwhelming the odds may seem.

My search for a wife has been like exploring an endless sandy seashore to find a small, priceless diamond. We have all been told that the priceless jewel called love does exist. But there are times when finding love seems impossible. I am one of those hopeful romantic explorers searching for that priceless jewel we call true love. Still, there are times when hopeful romantics like me surge forward with relentless passion and defy the odds. These hopeful romantics are fueled by an unquenchable thirst and an unrelenting hunger that can only be filled by love itself.

Although love seekers get emotionally hungry, they are never spiritually famished because they are nourished by an unseen food. Love explorers are driven by the reality that God is able to design someone just for them. They are not put off by the price they may have to pay to find this precious gift.

In my search, I have found that finding true love reminds me of a parable of a young man invited to return home to his deceased father's family estate. The grand old estate was located amidst an array of tall trees that danced in the wind. All the buildings featured striking architectural design and majestic flair. In the distance was a breathtaking beach featuring sparkling, pearly white sand with pink undertones. The water was a calming crystal blue.

A few days after his arrival, the young man was summoned to a private area of the beach. As the young man enjoyed the scenery, a stranger approached him and introduced himself as the longtime caretaker of his father's estate. The caretaker shared why his father invited him to the estate as the two men admired the scenery together.

He then told the young man that his father had left him special instructions to share with his son, and that he had eagerly awaited the day when the young man would arrive. The caretaker then started giving the young man specific instructions on how to find precious gemstones. He was there the day the young man's father buried in the sand the most beautiful diamond he had ever seen, just for his son.

After hearing this exciting news, the young man's emotions quickly ran the gamut. At first, he felt a burst of excitement and an eruption of curiosity. But then he quickly became painfully aware of the unfavorable odds of actually finding a diamond in so much sand. The young man concluded that the probability of finding one diamond on a beach full of sand was virtually impossible.

Noticing his distress, the caretaker gently placed his weathered hands on the young man's slumping shoulders. The older man and young man stood facing each other in suspended silence. After a few minutes passed, the caretaker tenderly assured him that his search would not be impossible if he followed his father's instructions. Then he began sharing words of wisdom.

"First," he said, "you must carefully study every one of your father's maps of the beach. You must become so familiar with them that you are able to reproduce them from memory. Second, when you get weary in your search, you must trust the maps because they will lead you to your diamond hidden in the sand. Finally, and most importantly, listen to the voice inside yourself. Listen to your inner voice because it will lead you through the sand and guide you toward your perfect diamond . . . of love."

Lessons from the Diamond in the Sand

Brother, I can hear you groaning already. You're thinking, *Pastor, that's a great story, but how can I really apply it to my life as a single man?* I'll tell you.

Lesson One: Respect God as Your Heavenly Father

As previously stated, the most important decision a man can make is to find the right God. As Christians we believe God is the creator and the essence of unconditional love. We can rest assured that God has the divine ability to create beautiful, godly women who are priceless.

The next critical life choice a man must make is to find the right wife. Just as the father in this story left his son with instructions to find the hidden treasure, God our Father has divinely left us with an internal road map that will lead every man to the right wife in due time.

Lesson Two: Allow the Son to Light Your Path

Ephesians 5:26-27 (NKJV) says Jesus is looking for his church, "that He might present her to Himself a glorious church, not having spot, or wrinkle, or any such thing, but that she should be holy and without blemish." This ideal is what every man should look for in a woman. Now, this doesn't mean she will be perfect—she is human. (It is the man's job to help perfect her with his love.)

Lesson Three: Make Room for the Holy Spirit to Comfort You on Your Journey

The Holy Spirit, our comforter, will lead and guide us into all truth. Just as the caretaker assisted the young man in his search for the priceless diamond, the Holy Spirit can lead us to women we can treasure. The Holy Spirit has the ability to lead us beyond the carnal desires of our flesh, and into the deepest desires of our hearts.

Lesson Four: Allow the Word of God to Guide Your Footsteps

Hebrews 4:12 (NKJV) says, "For the word of God is living and powerful, and sharper than any two-edged sword, piercing even to the division of soul and spirit, and of joints and marrow, and is a discerner of the thoughts and intents of the heart." God's Holy Word sets the definitive standard for love and manhood. The Word of God has the supernatural ability to help us discern our innermost thoughts and desires.

Lesson Five: Your Diamond Is Waiting for You

So often we use Proverbs 31 as a Bible-based behavioral template for Christian women. However, I believe this scripture can also serve as the ultimate, Bible-based template for identifying a godly woman.

Earlier, we saw how often people point out that we will never find the perfect woman. First, let me underscore the fact that most people understand in earnest there are no perfect people. However, if we can find a Proverbs 31 woman, we will get as close to perfection as humanly possible.

The Role of the Husband: The Nuts and Bolts of "I Do" for Men

Ephesians 5:25 (NKJV) commands men to "love your wives, just as Christ loved the church and gave himself up for her." Men must start the process of loving their wives before meeting them. I know this sounds radical, but take a moment to think about it. Ephesians 6:4 refers to the man as the bridegroom.

Therefore, the man must follow the example of Jesus by doing the following three critical things.

1. Put Your Past in a Coffin

The first thing a man must do to prepare for marriage is die to his past. Christ died for us so that the church could be born. A single man who is led by the Holy Spirit will start the process of dying to his past relationships long before his wife-to-be is birthed into his life. This crucifixion of his flesh is necessary in order to cleanse a man from his past negative proclivities so he can enter his marriage with a clean slate.

2. Bury Your Past in a Grave . . . and Don't Dig It Up Again!

The single man who is committed to being in a healthy marriage must be serious about burying the good, the bad, and the ugly he has encountered in past relationships. By burying his past, he will reduce the probability of comparing his future wife with women from his past. No woman wants to be compared to another woman, so this process is extremely important. When single men bury the ghosts from relationships past, they are able to give themselves completely to marriage.

3. Resurrect Yourself as a New Man

After Christ died and was resurrected, he appeared to over 500 people in his glorified body. In addition to having a new body, he took on a new behavior. His appearance and behavior were so radically different that Mary, one of his closest followers, did not recognize him at first sight. A single man who is serious about preparing for marriage will go through the process of death and burial in order to be resurrected with a radical change in behavior and appearance.

After Christ's resurrection, he gathered his followers together and told them he would not leave them comfortless. Then, he ascended into heaven to prepare their new home. Likewise, a godly single man will be motivated to start the process of preparing a home for his potential bride.

The purpose of this spiritual commitment is to cleanse the man from society's negative stimuli. Remember, just saying the words, "I Do" is no guarantee that an individual will perform the actions necessary to give life to the words. When a single man is truly committed to God's plan for marriage, he is willing to commit to all three truths without compromise. He will die to his past, bury his sins, and arise as a new man.

The Roles of a Godly Husband

As he prepares for marriage, the ultimate goal of a single man is to become the priest, provider, and protector for his wife and family. This process takes time, effort, and spiritual guidance.

The Priest

Hebrews 4:15 (NKJV) says, "We do not have a High Priest who cannot sympathize with our weaknesses, but was in all points tempted as we are, yet without sin." In the same manner, the man should be able to empathize with his wife's struggles, and like Jesus, prayerfully intercede on her behalf.

The beauty of this passage is that Jesus understands our search for future wives because he is searching for his ultimate bride, the church. We can count on Jesus as our example of how and what to choose in our future wives.

> MEN, WE MUST LEARN TO LOOK TO JESUS AS OUR COACH BECAUSE HE IS RIGHT THERE IN THE GAME WITH US.

When a single man desires to be married, he must follow the example of Christ in order to become a strong, godly priest.

The Provider

The Bible gives clear instructions to husbands about the importance of providing for the overall needs of their families. First Timothy 5:8 (NKJV) speaks of the importance of men providing for their families as he writes, "But if anyone does not provide for his own, and especially for those of his household, he has denied the faith and is worse than an unbeliever."

Timothy uses strong, direct language to describe men who fail as providers. He says men who fail to provide are worse than those who do not believe in God. This can be an overwhelming challenge for men at times. Nevertheless, with hard work and fervent prayer, the task of providing for our families can be achieved.

This is not to say that wives cannot help with the responsibilities of providing for the family. However, this responsibility rests primarily on the husband. Therefore, men should start the process of preparing to be a good provider long before marriage.

The Protector

Although some people say chivalry is dead in our modern culture, most women still seek their proverbial "knight in shining armor," and most men still desire to be knights for their queens. According to many surveys, one of the strongest needs for women in marriage is to feel protected. It is extremely important for men to give their women an environment of safety and protection.

Men must start the process of proverbial knighthood long before they get to the altar. A godly man must strive with all his might and pray with all his heart to be a sufficient protector for his wife and family.

The Parable of The Diamond In The Sand
Summing It All Up

A few years ago, I had the pleasure of performing a wedding for a beautiful young couple. Early on in the premarital sessions, I realized how committed the groom was to being an Ephesians 5 man. During the wedding ceremony, he demonstrated his commitment in a way I have never seen before.

On the day of the wedding, the groom requested to meet with me for a few minutes before the ceremony. In our brief meeting, he told me he wanted his bride and everything and everyone that was a part of her world. As we ended the meeting, he told me he had something special planned that was not rehearsed. I said, "Okay, it's your wedding."

Immediately after the couple exchanged their rings, the groom stepped forward and surprised everyone. He left the stage and placed a ring on the fingers of each of her children.

Tears flowed throughout the church as this young man declared his unconditional love for his bride and her children. Through that loving gesture, he told his bride he wanted to love her the way Christ loves his church.

When it comes to single men, I have discovered most of them dream of marrying the perfect woman. Many Christian men dream of marrying a Proverbs 31 woman. However, the following question must be asked:

> IF YOU WANT A PROVERBS 31 WOMAN, HOW ARE YOU STRIVING TO BE AN EPHESIANS 5 MAN?

If that is not your personal mission, I challenge you to start the process! If you are on that mission, I applaud you!

Summing it all up, if you are searching for your beautiful diamond in the sand, I am cheering you on. There may be challenges along the way, but don't give up and don't settle for less than God's best. The young man you just read about did not give up. He pressed through time and space, and ultimately married his childhood sweetheart.

In your meantime, it is my prayer that you will be strong and courageous as you search for love. As you move forward, go with the following assurances: first, God knows the kind of wife you need, so trust him; second, God wants you to find her, so keep searching; and third, God wants you to be ready for her, so allow him to mold you into the priest, provider, and protector for the special woman God has for you.

CHAPTER EIGHT

LEARNING TO DATE GOD'S WAY

*U*p to this point, you have been exposed to two of our core strategies for acknowledging who you are as a single person, and adjusting your lifestyle to God's will for your life. In the next two chapters you will gain strategies and learn the importance of activating a Bible-based plan to enjoy a healthy and fulfilled lifestyle as a single Christian.

Having facilitated countless singles conferences, I have been hit with many challenging questions from singles. However, the two most common questions I am asked are about sex and dating. In most cases, these questions come from non-Christians, new Christians, or Christians looking for some kind of excuse to sin.

Below you will find a list of other questions I hear most often in conferences and training settings. To keep it interesting, I will stagger these questions:

1. Is sex a sin?
2. Should I date or just pray and wait on God to send someone my way?
3. What does the Bible say about sex?

4. What does the Bible say about dating?
5. How can sex be wrong if I truly love someone?
6. Shouldn't I try things out so I can be sure we are sexually compatible?
7. Is it wrong for me to date an unbeliever?

In some seminars and conferences, at times, I have had to defer some of these questions to a female speaker or trained therapist in order to maintain my integrity and not exceed my skill set.

Learning to Date God's Way

As Christians, we are commanded to adhere to the principles of God's Word. When we are committed to dating God's way, the main goal should be to gather information on the possibility of becoming spiritually intimate versus gathering information on how to become physically intimate. The following parameters will give you concrete tools for dating according to a biblical standard, and steps for how to operate within each phase.

The Five Stages of Godly Dating

A successful, godly dating life can be achieved when we commit ourselves to the following stages:

- Sensational
- Emotional
- Social
- Initial Assessment
- Initial Commitment

The Sensational Stage: The Attraction

The Sensational Stage, or initial attraction, starts when your interest in another person is aroused. During this stage, the five senses often escalate to an extremely high level of awareness. When a man first sees, hears, touches, or smells a woman, he can feel like sparks are flying from his heart. Men are often more inspired by what they see before other senses are affected.

The Emotional Stage: The Feelings

The Emotional Stage is the period when feelings start to manifest. This stage is critical, especially early in the development of the relationship. In some instances, this stage may start relatively quickly. In other cases, budding emotions may develop at a slower pace based on sensory stimulation and personality type. A relationship that develops too quickly is like a microwave oven that produces instant, but short-lived results. The initial excitement of being attracted to another person often overshadows the excitement of developing a new relationship. The emotions might get hot, but they cool off just as fast.

You want to treat this period like a slow-cooking crockpot. A relationship that develops slowly provides the man and woman the opportunity to objectively evaluate their emotions. Couples can then give each other emotional space to allow the relationship to develop naturally.

The Social Stage: The Dating Period

The Social Stage, or dating period, is normally determined by the emotional intensity felt by the couple. If sensational and emotional levels are not solid, the social activities may dissolve just as quickly. During this stage, the relationship can evolve or dissolve with equal intensity based on the couple's social, spiritual, and cultural compatibilities.

While some relationships take off like rockets and soar into a romantic orbit, others prove to be mere infatuation or emotional flings. If attraction and feelings develop slowly, a successful, healthy, maturing relationship can happen. Planning a variety of activities in different settings allows a couple to gain a clearer understanding of their potential mate's true personality.

The Initial Assessment Stage: The First Reality Check

One of the essential reasons for dating is to gather data. Therefore, the Initial Assessment stage, or first reality check, is a pivotal point in determining the direction, definition, and destination of the relationship. During this stage, the first three levels of godly dating are separately and collectively assessed. The purpose of this initial assessment is to determine the following:

- The validity of the sensory level to determine the *direction* of the relationship

- The legitimacy of the emotional level to determine the *definition* of the relationship

- The social level to determine the **destination** of the relationship

This initial assessment becomes the first major reality check in the relationship. Every healthy relationship needs periodic assessments to maintain and ensure duration of the union.

The Initial Commitment Stage: The Engagement Period

The final stage of dating is the initial commitment stage or engagement period. At this point, the single man receives confirmation from God that he is with the woman God has designed for him. He will step up to the plate and put a ring on her finger. It is important to note that this step requires continued prayer, spiritual guidance, and commitment to preserving the woman in preparation for marriage.

Wait Until the Wait Is Over

Throughout the book, we explored various personalities and dating styles. I purposely saved Mr. and Ms. Caterpillar for last. The journey of Mr. and Ms. Caterpillar is taken directly from God's divine order of nature. This lesson is extremely important because so many people make the mistake of trying to force or speed up the process of marriage. Pay close attention so you can understand God's plan for your ultimate mate.

One day, a little boy was playing outside and came upon a caterpillar. After finding it, he immediately rushed home to show his mother what he had found. Excited about his new find, the boy asked his mother if he could keep it. The boy's mother permitted him to keep the caterpillar only if he promised to take care of it.

The boy cared for his new pet carefully until one day when he noticed the caterpillar acting differently. The boy panicked, but his mother reassured him the caterpillar was simply creating a cocoon. She explained that the caterpillar was preparing for metamorphosis so it could become a butterfly.

At first, the boy was excited about watching the caterpillar go through its changes. However, he soon became concerned because the butterfly was struggling so hard to get out. In an act of desperate compassion, the boy decided to get a pair of scissors, so he could help the butterfly break out of the cocoon.

When the butterfly came out, the boy was surprised. Its body was swollen, and its wings were small and shriveled up. The butterfly spent the rest of its life crawling around with a disfigured body. Sadly, the butterfly would never do what it was born to do—FLY.

From this experience, the boy learned a powerful lesson. In order for the butterfly to reach its optimum potential, it needed to go through the complete process, particularly that of struggling to free itself from the cocoon.

> WHEN COUPLES RUSH INTO MARRIAGE—WHEN THEY RUSH THE PROCESS—THE MARRIAGE PRODUCED CAN BE LIKE A DEFORMED BUTTERFLY.

The marriage does not morph into what it was designed to be. From my own personal journey, I must admit the process of waiting for love is not always easy. However, when I talk to happily married couples, they all say the wait that brought them together was worth it. Conversely, unhappy couples always say they wish they had waited.

Isaiah 40:31 (NKJV) says, "But they that wait upon the Lord shall renew their strength; they shall mount up with wings as eagles; they shall run, and not be weary; and they shall walk, and not faint." The best thing we can do as single people is wait until the wait is over. We cannot allow people, situations, and other circumstances to cause us to rush out of our cocoons of singlehood until the process is over. Coming out too soon will hinder us and those we date from being all we can be in relationships, and ultimately, marriage.

> I HAVE LEARNED THAT LIMITED PEOPLE FORM LIMITED RELATIONSHIPS. HURTING PEOPLE FORM HURTING RELATIONSHIPS. MOST IMPORTANTLY, SPIRITUALLY WEAK PEOPLE FORM SPIRITUALLY WEAK RELATIONSHIPS. TAKE YOUR TIME AND WAIT UNTIL THE WAIT IS OVER!

Three Steps to a Victorious Single Life

My final assignment is designed to help you do the following:

- Acknowledge who you are as a single person

- Adjust your lifestyle to God's will for your life

- Activate your God-inspired plan to enjoy a healthy and fulfilled lifestyle as a single Christian

---

STEP 1
I will take the following steps to acknowledge who I am as a single person:

_____

_____

_____

_____

STEP 2
I will take the following steps to adjust my life to God's plan:

_____

_____

_____

_____

STEP 3
I will take the following steps to activate my godly action plan:

_____

_____

_____

_____

CHAPTER NINE

DATING FOR DATA

*"No one is in charge of your happiness except you.
Therefore, don't allow anyone into the secret chambers of
your heart who does not have your best interests at heart."*
~Hiawatha Hemphill

*F*inding that special person to love can be like finding a needle in a haystack. I can't tell you how many times I have seen singles become so desperate for love that they just settle for the first sign of it they find.

To be honest, many times I have been tempted to compromise my standards and settle. But settling would be the worst thing I or anyone else could do when it comes to finding a life partner.

> THE ONLY THING WORSE THAN BEING SINGLE
> AND SAD IS BEING MARRIED AND MISERABLE.

Therefore, as singles we must sound the alarm, hold up the banner, and commit to believing—WE WILL NOT SETTLE FOR LESS THAN GOD'S BEST!

In this chapter, we will address one of the biggest mistakes many singles make when dating—allowing their need to be loved to overrule their need to get data about people they date. There are times when the desire to love and be loved can cause singles to deny reality and settle for someone who can never make them completely happy.

When we allow our need to be loved to overrule the reality of a bad relationship, we open the door to settling for less than God's best. However, there is a solution. I believe this process can be avoided once singles understand a simple concept I call, "Dating for Data." If you are ready to change, I invite you to explore, embrace, and implement this concept.

Dating for Data Defined

According to the Merriam-Webster's Dictionary[1], *data* is defined as "factual information used as a basis for reasoning, discussion, or calculation." As you read through this chapter, keep in mind these words: reasoning, discussion, and calculation. These words will be your guide as we go through the process of dating to gain data (information).

Reasoning, discussion, and calculation can serve as effective safe guards against committing to dead-end relationships, if you pay attention. I can't stress this enough: these words are your armor. No matter how attracted you are to the person, you must somehow come out of the romantic fog and develop healthy habits of reciprocal reasoning, honest discussion, and unbiased calculation with the person you are dating.

As stated above, Webster's Dictionary defines data as reasoning, discussion, and calculation. From these action words, we can begin the process of Dating for Data. Let's begin with Step One.

Step One: Reasoning— Approaching the Data Objectively

Lead with the Facts, Not Your Feelings

American motivational speaker and author Earl Nightingale talks about the importance of being reasonable in his successful audio book, *Lead the Field*.[2] Nightingale reports on a study that was done on the world's most successful people. One of the common threads found throughout this group of people was the ability to be reasonable. Leading with the facts versus leading with your feelings is the underpinning to Dating for Data. Leading with the facts is necessary because, so often, people approach new relationships looking for a romantic experience instead of trying to get to know the other person.

When dealing with the affairs of the heart, it is so easy to go into a romantic fog that is void of reality. Therefore, being reasonable is an important tool to temper your emotions. In addition, when you remain reasonable with yourself and the person you are dating, it becomes easier to deal with reality.

LET THE FACTS MOTIVATE YOUR FEELINGS!

Step Two: Discussion—Amplifying the Data Objectively

Let Them Talk Without Restriction
One of the biggest dating mistakes you can make is to set limits on what you want to hear about the person. Many people set these boundaries in place because of experiences that have hurt them in the past. As a result, you can actually start coaching your dates on what you can handle hearing. Big mistake!

> BY TRYING TO PROTECT YOURSELF FROM PAST HURTS, YOU ARE PROHIBITING YOURSELF FROM HEARING NEEDED INFORMATION FOR PRESENT AND FUTURE DISCUSSIONS.

When I say allow people to speak without restriction, I'm not saying you should allow people to speak to you disrespectfully. When a person speaks to you disrespectfully, that is usually a precursor to disrespectful behavior to follow. Disrespect on any level is not only a red flag, it is what I call a burning red flag that should not be ignored.

Nevertheless, don't restrict people to the point where they are not allowed to identify themselves. You are limiting yourself from gaining important information you need to know before you allow yourself to get too involved emotionally. Proverbs 4:23 (NIV) says, "Above all else, guard your heart, for everything you do flows from it." Many singles actually think they are guarding their hearts by coaching a person's speech. However, singles who coach or limit open discussion, in many cases, also limit themselves on how much they can express their needs and expectations to those they date. Limited discussion leads to limited information, which can lead to a limited relationship.

From personal experience, I have discovered that when you do not allow for truthful, open discussion, over time, the truth will eventually come out one way or another. Remember, it's better to hear and state the truth early on so you can discuss the deal breakers before you are emotionally attached, sharing a child, or married.

Amp it up SO YOU CAN GET THE FACTS UP FRONT!

LISTEN WITHOUT RESTRICTION, AND LET HIM OR HER LISTEN TO YOU WITHOUT RESTRICTION

After you have resolved within yourself to allow the person you are dating to talk without restrictions, you should be willing to actively listen, without restriction. New Testament writer, James, provides us with information on the importance of effective listening as he instructs us to be "quick to listen, slow to speak, and slow to get angry" (James 1:19 NLT).

In his book, *Seven Habits of Highly Effective People*, internationally acclaimed author Dr. Steven R. Covey[3] suggests we should "seek first to understand, then to be understood." The concept of seeking first to understand is extremely important because most people do not know how to effectively listen, in general.

When you add the need for listening in a dating relationship, the ability to listen can become even more challenging because emotions are involved. This problem usually arises because both people are trying to get their point across. Consequently, in order to have a healthy relationship, both people must learn to listen without restrictions.

According to Covey, the root of ineffective listening is that "Most people do not listen with the intent to understand; they listen with the intent to reply. They're filtering everything through their own paradigms, reading their autobiography into other people's lives."

Both the secular and sacred scholars point to the importance of healthy listening and objectively processing what you are hearing. By allowing an open, honest, and two-fold healthy discussion in the dating process, we open the door to move forward.

Amp it up, LISTEN WITHOUT RESTRICTION!

Step Three: Calculation—Approaching the Data

Measure the Data Against Your Emotions

Once you have embraced the importance of allowing yourself and others to talk without restrictions, and allowing yourself and others to listen without restrictions, it is time to assess the information.

In May 1961, the late, great R&B singer Marvin Gaye debuted his first single, "Let Your Conscience Be Your Guide."[4] The first line of the song says, "Let your conscience be your guide, it won't lie to you." Over fifty years later, these words are as true and profound as the day they were written, and have become a popular colloquialism in our culture.

In light of the song's lyrical content, the following question comes to mind: What is the fuel that feeds the conscience? INFORMATION. The information received by the conscience guides the thoughts. In turn, the conscience guides the actions.

This is why is it so important to get as much information as possible up front about a person to whom you are attracted.

Conduct a Benjamin Franklin

Benjamin Franklin, one of America's founding fathers, implemented a detailed chart designed to compare the pros and cons when making major decisions. Today, many people still use the Benjamin Franklin method of checks and balances when making important decisions.

So, can the Benjamin Franklin method of checks and balances apply to dating? Absolutely! When we are hungry for love, our emotions can become uncontrollable. Second, when we meet someone to whom we are extremely attracted, our emotions can be easily deceived. Third, when we meet someone who has a surplus of emotional baggage, the vulnerable areas of our heart can be innocently pulled into an unhealthy situation or relationship.

Using the Benjamin Franklin Chart for Dating Data

Sample Relationship #1

Bill and Sheila have dated for six months. The relationship is in limbo because they have not mutually given the relationship any definition. Bill wants to take the relationship to the next level, while Sheila is not sure if she is ready to make that kind of commitment.

As you can see, Bill and Sheila both need to conduct a Benjamin Franklin Chart in order to assess how they will proceed. Remember, this is critical because when we ignore the facts and rely on our feelings, one or both people can suffer unnecessary pain.

BILL AND SHEILA'S BENJAMIN FRANKLIN CHART

The Facts	*The Feelings*
Dated for six months	Bill has strong feelings for Sheila
The relationship is in limbo	Bill wants a romantic relationship with Sheila
Sheila is not ready to move forward	

Sample Relationship #2

Mark and Kelly have dated for a year. The relationship is more of a friendship; however, Kelly wants more. The problem is Mark still has many unresolved issues from his past and is not ready to commit to a serious relationship.

MARK AND KELLY'S BENJAMIN FRANKLIN CHART

The Facts	*The Feelings*
Dated for one year	Kelly wants more from Mark
The relationship is in limbo	Mark has unresolved past issues
Mark is not ready to move forward	

The Result of the Sample Benjamin Franklin

Both couples should make some serious adjustments before moving forward. Moving forward without knowing and dealing with the facts can result in hurt, frustration, and disappointment because they are dealing with affairs of the heart.

The Benefits of Dating for Data

Healthy dating is far more than just an emotional experience. It is human nature for our emotions to be stimulated when we are attracted to someone. Nevertheless, we cannot allow nature to cloud the data we discover about the people we date. Therefore, it is imperative that, as we gather data, we keep our emotions in check.

At the end of the day, we come to the realization that our emotions can be fickle. On the other hand, hard data about the person you are dating is objectively factual. Therefore, dating to gather accurate data in the relationship is extremely important. It helps singles do the following:

- Recognize the warning signs at the entry point of the relationship
- Be alert to the warning signs as they surface during the relationship
- Accept or reject the person's past and present
- Identify deal breakers early in the relationship
- Define the relationship early enough for both parties to have a pleasant experience

- Make a decision to sustain or end the romantic elements of the relationship on a positive note (Sometimes these resolutions can evolve into a healthy platonic friendship.)
- Transition the relationship into its proper status

A Final Thought on Dating for Data

Now that you have been introduced to Dating for Data, it's time to get out and meet other singles. As you meet other singles, remember you are dating first and foremost to get to know the other person. Getting emotionally involved too quickly can cause you to miss critical red flags you need to see. As a final point, with God we never have to settle for less. However, sometimes we do have to wait in order to receive his best!

CHAPTER TEN

PREMARITAL SEX—THE X FACTOR

*R*ecently, I had a conversation with a friend of mine. During that conversation, he told me he had read a blog[1] on the negative effects of premarital sex. As the conversation progressed, he started to give me some interesting details from the blog post.

The main theme of the blog focused on how males leave their DNA inside their partners during sex. My friend went on to tell me that the blog detailed the many negative spiritual, emotional, and physical side effects that women and men experience as DNA is exchanged during premarital sex.

Near the end of the conversation, my friend became extremely remorseful. Then he ended the conversation by saying something to this effect: "If I could turn back the hands of time, I would have never had sex before marriage—I wish I had waited." Overwhelmed by all this information, I simply responded, "I guess that's the purpose of grace."

As a single Christian, there is a vigorous struggle to live a life of purity. You are in an all-out war with the natural desire to feel, touch, smell, hear, and even taste unconditional love. However, you can take courage in the reality that "no temptation has overtaken you except such as is common to man; but God is faithful, who will not allow you to be tempted beyond what you are able, but with the temptation will also make the way of escape, that you may be able to bear it" (1 Corinthians 10:13 NKJV).

In this chapter we will look at one of the biggest struggles Christian singles face—PREMARITAL SEX! It is the proverbial elephant in the room. Many singles talk about their never-ending struggle to abstain from sex before marriage. Even though this issue can be challenging, you must remember the availability of God's grace.

According to *Dictionary.com*, "*X factor*"[2] is defined as a "hard-to-describe influence or quality with unknown consequences." The term is often used to describe public figures such as entertainers or athletes gifted with extraordinary, yet hard-to-describe talents.

More specifically, premarital sex is the X factor for four primary reasons. First, premarital sex has devastating physical effects that can be life-changing or even life-ending. Second, premarital sex has unhealthy emotional effects that can be hard to overcome. Third, premarital sex has long-range negative relational effects that can extend into future relationships, including marriage. Fourth, and most important, premarital sex severely affects a single's spiritual relationship with God.

Sex between two married people was ordained by God as early as the Garden of Eden. Fast forward to the New Testament and you will find God continues to encourage limiting sex to the marriage bed. The author of the New Testament book of Hebrews describes sex in marriage as being honorable and undefiled.

The apostle Paul warns of the consequences of engaging in premarital sex in 1 Corinthians 6:18 (NIV) as follows: "Flee from sexual immorality. All other sins a person commits are outside the body, but whoever sins sexually, sins against their own body." Notice Paul points out that those who engage in sexual immorality do not only bring destruction to their partners, but destroy their own bodies as well.

THE NEGATIVE EFFECTS OF PREMARITAL SEX

Unhealthy Physical Effects

Sexually Transmitted Diseases

Premarital sex can result in many unhealthy physical side effects. The first unhealthy physical side effect we will look at is the risk of contracting sexually transmitted diseases. There are various marketing campaigns that promote safe sex. However, there are no proof positive ways to tell if a person has a sexually transmitted disease without a medical examination. Abstinence is the only real safe sex.

Pregnancy

The second unhealthy physical side effect of premarital sex is the risk of premarital pregnancy. In addition to the possibility of contracting a sexually transmitted disease, pregnancy is always a possibility—even when using contraception.

In Genesis 1:28 (NKJV), God commanded Adam and Eve to "be fruitful and multiply; fill the earth and subdue it." Notice he gives the charge to have children to a married couple. Great joy comes with childbirth; however, pregnancies outside the marriage bond tend to pose many challenges.

Unmarried Co-Parenting

Unmarried pregnancy sets in motion a chain of events that bind two people together. The binding of two people who share children, but are not married to each other, is more often than not more challenging than expected.

One of the worst-case scenarios is to have to share custody with an abusive, unsupportive, or unloving co-parent. In these kinds of situations, sharing children can be emotionally, physically, and financially draining for the dedicated parent.

In abusive relationships where co-parenting is involved, the abuser tends to control nearly every aspect of the victimized parent's life. As a result, the victim's life can become frozen because of intimidation and control inflicted on them by the abusive parent.

Interestingly, the abusive co-parent not only controls the victim but also indirectly controls everyone associated with the victim, including family, friends, and even potential dating partners. Unfortunately, because of the controlling nature of the abuser, the co-parenting victim can have difficulty establishing and maintaining healthy relationships. Tragically, there are times when this abuse ends in death.

Abortion

There is great disagreement about abortion in today's society. Nevertheless, abortion is another unhealthy side effect of premarital sex. Author Michael Snyder states in his blog post, entitled *19 Facts About Abortion in America That Should Make You Very Sick,*[3] that every day in America more than 3,000 babies are aborted. Whether you are pro-life or pro-abortion, you can clearly see from the above information that abortion is disturbing.

Still, there is a solution that can only be found in God's Word. Psalm 127:3 (NIV) says, "Children are a heritage from the LORD, offspring a reward from him." Wess Stafford, President Emeritus of Compassion International says, "Every child you encounter. . . is a divine appointment."[4]

Unhealthy Emotional Effects

A close friend's sister had hopes of sharing a beautiful life with her childhood sweetheart. During the good times of their relationship, they had a beautiful baby girl, but they never married. As a co-parent, he has broken her heart and their child's heart over and over again.

The emotional consequences of premarital sexual involvement are damaging on many levels. In fact, the unhealthy physical effects of premarital sex often flow into unhealthy emotional effects. Unwed and unwanted pregnancy becomes an emotional strain on parents and children. Unproductive co-parenting can also cause irreparable emotional issues. Abortions can also cause great emotional pain for many women later in life.

In conversations with singles, I have discovered that premarital sex can lead to regret, emotional emptiness, and many of other long-range negative behaviors. Emotional issues related to sex are primarily prompted by ungodly thoughts. It is a natural progression for our emotions to be touched by our experiences.

When it comes to sex, the thoughts and activities are stored just as a computer stores information on its hard drive. Once thoughts and activities are conceived, they are converted into what some refer to as mental flashbacks. A mental flashback can bring up previous sexual experiences. Remarkably, these flashbacks can occur any time, at any place—even at church.

If that has happened to you, it doesn't mean you're irreparably depraved or that God's grace is insufficient. It simply means you are human.

In light of the fact that sexual encounters usually involve all five senses, mental flashbacks can become even harder to break. The main problem with reoccurring mental flashbacks is that they leave individuals with pain, mistrust, guilt, and a myriad of other toxic emotional thoughts. These thoughts can be vivid and occur frequently.

UNHEALTHY RELATIONAL EFFECTS

Not only does premarital sex have unhealthy, negative physical and emotional effects, it also has unhealthy relationship effects. One of the negative social effects of premarital sex is the inability to develop and maintain healthy Christian relationships.

In the past, when a young man was interested in dating a young lady, the young man would actually have to get the approval of the family. The dates were strictly chaperoned. In some cultures, the family was so involved in the courtship process that the marriage was actually arranged by the family.

In today's liberal American culture, the moral stance for sexual purity has been significantly relaxed. Dating standards have diminished to the point where there is a style of dating called "friends with benefits." In this kind of relationship, there is no meaningful or intimate relational connection. The relationship is based solely on sex. The underlying problem in these relationships is that the sexual act becomes the focus rather than the people or the relationship.

As a minister, I have talked to many men and women who complain of the deep regret they have felt after looking back on their premarital sexual experiences. I have talked with women who viewed sex as an emotional connection rather than just a casual physical act. In contrast, when talking with men, I have discovered they view sex as a pleasurable physical experience more than an emotional connection. Even though women and men viewed sex differently, both sexes complained of the pain and unhealthy emotional residue of premarital sex.

UNHEALTHY MARITAL EFFECTS

The negative effects of premarital sex on relationships can extend into marriage. In his infinite wisdom, God masterfully designed marriage to be a loving union of trust and fidelity between two people. His original plan for marriage was that couples learn about sex together, after marriage. When couples follow God's plan and wait to have sex within marriage, they can create unforgettable memories without any interference from the past.

A perfect world populated by perfect people would operate in God's plan to perfection. However, we know that's not reality because we have all sinned in some way or another. As a result, marriage takes work. Marriage is the merging of two people, with two different personalities, who strive to be one.

When you add unresolved sexual issues from past relationships with personality and gender differences, the marital challenges become even greater. One of the main problems faced by couples who had multiple past sexual partners is they sometimes tend to start comparing their marital sex life to their premarital sex life. As you can clearly imagine, this can cause some serious problems.

Another added strain on the marital workload is premarital cohabitation. Proof of this is found in a *New York Times*[5] article written by clinical psychologist Meg Jay. In this article, Jay states that women typically use "cohabitation as a step toward marriage, while men are more likely to see it as a way to test a relationship or postpone commitment." This gender conflict often leads to unsatisfied marriages and even divorce.

UNHEALTHY SPIRITUAL EFFECTS

The apostle Paul alludes to the concept of healthy soul ties between married couples in Ephesians 5:31 (KJV), which says, "For this cause shall a man leave his father and mother, and shall be joined unto his wife, and they two shall be one flesh." This kind of soul tie was instituted and encouraged by God at the first marriage—that of Adam and Eve. The marriage of Adam and Eve provides us with the Bible-based template for healthy sex within a marriage.

In his infinite wisdom, God forbids premarital sex—not to punish us, but to protect us. The main problem with having premarital sex is that it creates an unhealthy bond between two people—a so-called soul tie. The phrase "soul tie" is a man-made concept used to describe a spiritual principle of connection. According to *urbandictionary.com*[6] a *soul tie* is "a spiritual/ emotional connection you have to someone after being intimate with them, usually when engaging in sexual intercourse."

Unfortunately, sexual soul ties have the ability to spiritually fragment the soul—especially in those who have experienced numerous sexual relationships. I have found that these individuals often find it very difficult to develop meaningful Christ-centered relationships because their souls are so fragmented.

The writer of Hebrews brings it all together by providing conclusive evidence on the difference between godly and ungodly soul ties. The writer tells us in Hebrews 13:4 (NKJV) that

"Marriage is honorable among all, and the bed undefiled; but fornicators and adulterers God will judge."

WINNING THE WAR AGAINST PREMARITAL SEX

I believe the best way to go forward is to realize that what you are leaving behind is not worth going back to. So, as you dedicate yourself to moving forward and living a life of sexual purity as a single, I encourage you to commit yourself to three words we discussed in a previous chapter: ACKNOWLEDGE, ADJUST, ACTIVATE.

ACKNOWLEDGE, ADJUST, and ACTIVATE are the foundation of our Bible-based battle strategy for winning the war against sexual immorality. They will also serve as our battle cry for living a life of hope and sexual purity. To be more specific, the battle strategy involves the following three steps:

1. Acknowledge the need to live a life of sexual purity.
2. Adjust your attitude to living a life of sexual purity.
3. Activate your game plan to live a life of sexual purity.

ACKNOWLEDGE THE NEED TO LIVE A LIFE OF SEXUAL PURITY

Today, we are literally bombarded with images that contain explicit sexual images on a daily basis. Books, movies, TV shows, and other media all condone and celebrate sexual immorality. Just the other day I saw a TV commercial about milk, and it was full of sexual overtones. I couldn't believe they had taken something as innocent as milk and tarnished its image with something so negative.

Back in the scarlet letter days (as referenced in *The Scarlet Letter* by Nathaniel Hawthorne[7]), sexual immorality was not tolerated. If a person was convicted of being sexually promiscuous, he or she would be ostracized and forced to wear a red letter of shame. In contrast, in today's culture people are ostracized for refraining from sex before marriage. The standards for sexual purity have been relaxed significantly since the days of the scarlet letter. As a result, many people—even Christians— see nothing wrong with sex outside of marriage.

These days, people have come up with all kinds of reasons to justify their involvement in sex before marriage. Some say it's okay to have premarital sex because they are involved in a long-term, loving relationship. Still others say it's okay as long as sex is consensual. Although these arguments may contain some elements of truth, they are still wrong according to the scriptures.

Romans 3:4 (NIV) says, "Let God be true, and every human being a liar." In this passage, the apostle Paul makes it clear that God's Word is the ultimate standard of righteousness and truth. Therefore, if God's Word says sex outside of marriage is wrong, then as Christians, we are to live by that standard.

Author and lecturer John C. Maxwell[8] says, "A man must be big enough to admit his mistakes, smart enough to profit from them, and strong enough to correct them." Premarital sex is no different. The first step to sexual purity is to acknowledge it is a mistake and be willing to correct the situation.

As you acknowledge that premarital sex is wrong, don't make the mistake of beating yourself up. Remember, God is not a spiritual patrol officer roaming the universe, looking for people to punish. God is far more loving and forgiving. First John 1:9 (ESV) assures us that "if we confess our sins, he is faithful and just to forgive us our sins and to cleanse us from all unrighteousness."

Listed below are ten Bible-based reasons why premarital sex is destructive to your overall well-being. As you read through the list, take time to resolve within yourself that sex outside marriage is wrong in the sight of God.

10 BIBLE-BASED REASONS NOT TO HAVE PREMARITAL SEX

1. Premarital sex is forbidden by God in scripture.
2. Premarital sex breaks our fellowship with God.
3. Premarital sex is a sin against our own bodies, which God designed to be temples of the Holy Spirit.
4. Premarital sex hurts our testimony as a believer.
5. Premarital sex leads to a hypocritical lifestyle.
6. Premarital sex causes guilt, shame, and unhealthy bonds between partners.
7. Premarital sex can cause ungodly thoughts that can extend into the future.
8. Premarital sex can cause unhealthy emotions that can extend into the future.
9. Premarital sex can lead to a lack of self-control that can extend into the future.
10. Premarital sex can lead to ungodly habits that can extend into a future marriage.

ADJUST YOUR MINDSET TO LIVING A LIFE OF SEXUAL PURITY AND DETOXING FROM YOUR SEXUAL PAST

After acknowledging that premarital sex is unhealthy and ungodly, it's time to adjust your thinking. It is time to commit to a lifestyle of sexual purity. In a previous chapter, we dealt with the importance of detoxing from past negativity. Now it's time to go through the process of detoxing from past sexual encounters.

When it comes to premarital sex, detoxing is critically important. The best way to stop doing something is to cleanse the system from the thing you are trying to overcome. For example, when substance abusers are admitted for treatment, they must first go through a detox program in order to get the substance out of their system. Premarital sex must be dealt with in the same manner. In order to stop it, we must get it out of our system.

I cannot overemphasize the importance of spiritually, mentally, and physiologically cleansing yourself from the sexual sins of your past. Detoxing from sexual immorality is critical according to the apostle Paul because it is a self-destructive sin against one's own body.

Listed below are detox scriptures and a detox affirmation designed to help strengthen you in your journey toward sexual purity.

DETOX SCRIPTURES

- "But fornication and all uncleanness or covetousness, let it not even be named among you, as is fitting for saints" (Ephesians 5:3 NKJV).

- "Marriage is honorable among all, and the bed undefiled; but fornicators and adulterers God will judge" (Hebrews 13:4 NKJV).

- "Beloved, I beg you as sojourners and pilgrims, abstain from fleshly lusts which war against the soul" (1 Peter 2:11 NKJV).

- "Nevertheless, because of sexual immorality, let each man have his own wife, and let each woman have her own husband" (1 Corinthians 7:2 NKJV).

- "Therefore put to death your members which are on the earth: fornication, uncleanness, passion, evil desire, and covetousness, which is idolatry" (Colossians 3:5 NKJV).

- "Flee sexual immorality. Every sin that a man does is outside the body, but he who commits sexual immorality sins against his own body" (1 Corinthians 6:18 NKJV).

- "Flee also youthful lusts; but pursue righteousness, faith, love, peace with those who call on the Lord out of a pure heart" (2 Timothy 2:22 NKJV).

- "Or do you not know that your body is the temple of the Holy Spirit who is in you, whom you have from God, and you are not your own" (1 Corinthians 6:19 NKJV)?

- "For this is the will of God, your sanctification: that you should abstain from sexual immorality that each of you should know how to possess his own vessel in sanctification and honor" (1 Thessalonians 4:3-4 NKJV).

DETOX AFFIRMATION FROM SEXUAL SINS

I will commit to going through the process of cleansing myself from the people, behaviors, and memories involved in past premarital sexual relationships. I will also commit to not talk or even think about those ungodly relationships. Most importantly, I will forgive myself of the past and move forward by faith toward my God-designed destiny.

It's not enough to ask God to forgive you—you must forgive yourself as well. The best way to forgive yourself is to see yourself as God sees you. The reason to forgive yourself is because God has forgiven you. The point here is, if God—who is sinless—is willing to forgive us, who are we to hold ourselves hostage to the sins of our past? Isaiah tells us, "Though your sins are like scarlet, they shall be as white as snow; though they are red like crimson, they shall be as wool" (Isaiah 1:18 NKJV).

ACTIVATE YOUR GAME PLAN FOR A LIFESTYLE OF SEXUAL PURITY

Now that you have processed the detox scriptures, the detox affirmation, and the ten reasons for not having premarital sex, it's time to take the final steps. It's time to activate your game plan to live a life of sexual purity. Activating your game plan will involve the following three changes in behavior:

1. Thinking about sex from a healthy biblical perspective.
2. Talking about sex in the future tense (post marriage).
3. Practicing a present and future tense lifestyle of sexual abstinence until marriage.

Wait! I hope I didn't lose you about remaining abstinent until marriage. Some people check out at that point. However, I pray that you will press forward. You are so close to reaching your goal.

PRESENT TENSE, GODLY SEX THINKING

As stated earlier, sex is all around us. It's almost impossible not to think about it. However, in order to jumpstart the process of activating your game plan to live a life of sexual purity, you must first and foremost change your way of thinking. Changing how you think about sex is imperative because of the soul ties, mental flashbacks, and other unhealthy habits you have developed from previous sexual experiences.

The apostle Paul tells us in Philippians 4:8 (NKJV), "Finally, brethren, whatever things are true, whatever things are noble, whatever things are just, whatever things are pure, whatever things are lovely, whatever things are of good report, if there is any virtue and if there is anything praiseworthy—meditate on these things." The main point to remember in the above passage is the importance of restricting your thoughts to ideas that have virtue and that are worthy of praise. In light of this, it is clear that we must change our thinking about sex. We must start to think about sex the way God created us to think about it. This is what I call present tense, godly sex thinking.

FUTURE TENSE, GODLY SEX TALK

Once you develop the habit of present tense, godly sex thinking, you are ready to start developing the habit of future tense, godly sex talk. The New Testament writer Luke tells us, "for his mouth speaks from the overflow of his heart" (Luke 6:45 AMP). Luke is telling us that the mouth is merely confirming what the heart contains.

When it comes to Christian dating, we must be careful how much and what kind of information we divulge—particularly when it comes to past sexual experiences. I have talked to many singles who complain about their dates telling them too much about their sexual past. For example, many singles who have not committed to a lifestyle of sexual purity make the dreaded mistake of talking candidly with new people about their sexual past.

Some singles go as far as to give explicit details about prior sexual encounters. I believe this kind of dialogue serves no spiritual nor practical purpose when trying to establish healthy boundaries in dating relationships. This kind of liberal dating can be a turnoff, particularly when people start involuntarily comparing previous sexual partners with a potential person of interest.

I've heard the argument, "If someone loves me, I should be able to tell them everything, including my sexual past." However, when we look at this from a practical and spiritual perspective, telling someone about something forbidden in scripture causes him or her to accept something God never ordained in the first place.

Sometimes people need to talk to someone about past hurtful sexual experiences. In this case, I suggest talking to a Christian counselor, pastor, or a trusted, spiritually mature person. By talking to someone other than the object of your affection, you can avoid future problems that can infiltrate the relationship.

The solution is to adopt the practice of what I call future tense, godly sex talk. Future tense, godly sex talk is the process of discussing sex after marriage. This kind of dialogue should only take place when a couple is engaged and headed to the marriage altar. The purpose is to establish each person's likes and dislikes without engaging in sex. The ultimate goal here is once couples are married, they can learn to please each other based on the desires of each rather than by replicating sexual experiences from the past.

LIVING A PRESENT AND FUTURE TENSE GODLY LIFESTYLE

When we give ourselves away in premarital sex, we are giving away physical, emotional, and spiritual pieces of ourselves to someone who does not belong to us. In short, we are committing the act of human trespassing, or what I call body invasion. When we do this, we are giving intimate pieces of ourselves and stealing intimate pieces of the other person.

In an article entitled *A Renewed Virginity*,[9] Christian counselors Drs. Greg and Michael Smalley write about the concept of "renewed virginity." The article concludes with the following powerful words of hope: "You can't change the past, but you can allow God to enter into your brokenness and give you what you need to honor His plan of sexuality." For Christians, the goal is to rededicate themselves to sexual purity until marriage. Committing to renewed virginity is a beautiful way to prepare yourself for a healthy sex life after marriage.

The first time I was exposed to the idea of recommitting to sexual purity was at a conference conducted by Dr. Edwin Cole. In his message, Dr. Cole told the audience that engaging in sex before marriage is to give someone your "uniqueness." As I processed what Dr. Cole was saying, I started to finally understand what God, my pastor, my grandmother, and every other wise person had been trying to tell me about the importance of sexual abstinence.

At the end of the service, Dr. Cole conducted an altar call allowing people to repent and reclaim their sexual purity. Almost immediately the altar was flooded with people. I couldn't help but notice that most of the people at that altar were young, beautiful women.

I was so profoundly overwhelmed by the guilt of my past that I couldn't move. So, I just sat there in my seat and took it all in. Young men and women were coming to the altar broken and ashamed. However, they were leaving that altar with a new hope and wholeness. Since that experience, I no longer see women as objects to sexually conquer, but as my spiritual sisters who deserve my respect.

THE DAY THE LIGHT CAME ON

After that service, the light came on for me concerning the seriousness of premarital sex. That day, God revealed to me that when we have premarital sex, we become like thieves who commit home invasions.

When a thief commits a home invasion, he or she usually ransacks the home and steals items that are precious to the owner. The thief leaves the owner broken and confused. Similarly, when we engage in premarital sex, we are breaking and entering into spaces forbidden by God. We are violating someone else and compromising ourselves.

No matter how much we may care about the other person, we are committing an unlawful invasion. No matter how good it may feel, we are still in violation of God's Word. No matter how right it may seem, we are trespassing in a forbidden area. No matter how much we may even love the other person, we are a thief nevertheless because we are ransacking someone's soul and stealing precious pieces of his or her spirit when we have premarital sex. HOWEVER, THERE IS HOPE!

THERE IS HOPE
When fate has dealt the pain,
And your heart feels the shame,
There is hope,
There is still hope in Christ.

These words are from a song I wrote during one of the darkest periods in my life. That experience, though devastating, brought me to a deeper revelation of just how much God loves me. Therefore, as I conclude this chapter, I encourage you to place your hope in the love of Jesus Christ. Finding hope in Christ is far more fulfilling than obsessively hoping to find a person or relationship to fulfill you.

Real hope as a single starts the moment you resolve within yourself that Christ is your first love. The next step toward real hope is to start loving yourself unconditionally. Until you have developed a deep love affair with God and yourself, you will never be able to sufficiently enjoy a love affair with another person.

In order to enjoy meaningful, Christian dating relationships, you must first understand you are God's human masterpiece. As you start to see yourself as God's masterpiece, you are able to look beyond the human flaws of others. The ability to look beyond the outward flaws of others empowers us to appreciate their inner beauty.

As you reach these thresholds, you win battles along the way toward sexual purity. With faith and determination, you will be able to move forward into meaningful relationships. As you immerse yourself in God's Word, you will be able to establish relationships that are anchored in God's "agape" love (Greek word for unconditional love) versus human "eros" love (Greek word for erotic love). With Christ, you will ultimately win the war over the X factor of premarital sex in your life.

Once I understood the many negative effects of premarital sex, I made a commitment to protect the women God placed in my path. In light of my commitment to sexual purity, I prayed that God would surround my future wife with people with that same level of commitment.

With this in mind, I can remember standing on a street corner in Pittsburgh, Pennsylvania. For some reason, all my friends had gone into the church and left me alone outside. While standing there on that chilly street corner, thoughts and questions concerning my future wife started to flood my mind. Questions like, *"Where is she, and is she safe?"* Suddenly, the thought that we could be sharing the same moonlight calmed me.

Out of nowhere, I was overwhelmed by an unanticipated moment of romantic hope. So I just stood there longing and praying for my future wife. The longer I stood there, the more my resolve for sexual purity was renewed. That night I could only dream of sharing the moonlight with her. Some day we will share sunlit days and moonlit nights for the rest of our lives.

CHAPTER ELEVEN

AN UNEXPECTED NUGGET OF WISDOM

"While positive words can inspire dreams,
negative words can shatter them."
~Hiawatha Hemphill

When I am introduced, people often describe me as being a single, never married, educated Christian man. To many people, that introduction sounds strange. As a result, some people may be prone to think something must be wrong with me. For some reason, when you are a single man, people often think of you as a player, gay, or someone with commitment issues.

Sometimes, after I am introduced, people will ask me the following question: How can a heterosexual, educated Christian man not be married? Oftentimes, the questions get worse. Once I crossed over the threshold of forty, people really started to think something had to be off kilter with me. It got so bad at one point that I just stopped telling people my age altogether.

There was a period in my life when I was constantly trying to offer reasons for my singleness. Day after day, I would find myself trying to explain why I was not married. More importantly, I was trying to explain to my critics that someday I would love to be married.

I really love women. But the constant negativity about my status became hurtful. Every time questions came up about my relationship status, I would cringe and wonder how people could be so insensitive.

Over time, I became more sensitive to the situations and circumstances of others. For example, I started noticing when people would ask married couples, "When are you going to have a baby?" Questions like this began to really annoy me. Suppose that couple was infertile and unable to have children? I felt questions like this were just as intrusive as asking about a person's relationship status. This type of questioning can come off as particularly cruel, especially when people desire to have that special someone God has designed just for them.

As time passed, my pain started escalating because I could not understand how people could be so blatantly insensitive. People were asking me to answer questions I could not even answer myself. They were asking me to give them reasons for not having what I so greatly desired.

However, between the pain and unfair questions, there has always been an unrelenting hope. You could say I am a hopeful romantic. This ever-present hope has kept me through my wilderness days—days when I just needed that special someone to love me back.

My struggle to deal with the uncomfortable questions continued until one day when I met an elderly businessman on a flight to the West coast. I could tell from the manner in which this man introduced himself that he was a talker. I could see he was the kind of person who was determined to make me a new friend, with or without my consent. Since I was exhausted from my hectic schedule, I thought the flight would be the perfect time to get in a much-needed power nap. However, my new friend had other ideas. The more I tried to position myself in that tiny airplane seat for my nap, the more determined he became to hold a conversation with me.

Ten minutes later, this gentleman was not taking the hint that I didn't want to be bothered. He was determined to engage me in conversation despite me closing my eyes and making vain attempts to get comfortable with the airline's flimsy loaner pillow. Since he was determined to talk with me, I just gave up and decided to keep the conversation going. I had rationalized that if I indulged this man for a little while, maybe he would leave me alone and I would eventually be able to take my nap.

As I engaged the man in conversation, he wasted no time popping the dreaded question, "Are you married?" I thought, *Oh no. Here we go again.* I predicted it was going to be a very long flight. By now, I was bracing myself for the whole, "Why are you still single?" question.

To my surprise, that was not how the conversation unfolded at all. When I finally revealed to him that I wasn't married, he dropped a nugget of wisdom into my heart that changed my life forever. He simply said, "It's better to want something you don't have, than to have something you don't want."

W-O-W!

If I had rudely blown him off, I would have missed that life-changing nugget. The life lesson here is there are special times in life when God uses unexpected encounters and unfamiliar people to stretch us so we can see life from a better vantage point. In fact, this powerful wisdom nugget has profoundly reshaped my life as a single man.

Even though I never saw the man again, he had given me a gift I feel obligated to pay forward to anyone willing to receive it. For all who are willing to receive this wisdom, I am honored to share it with you. What I have to share is a threefold message.

First, when you're feeling lonely and discouraged, I pray you will find strength in my story. Second, when unkind people flippantly chide you because you're still single, I encourage you to quickly detox those words and keep moving forward. Third, when the single life seems unbearable, hold fast to the wisdom nugget I received from a stranger:

> "IT'S BETTER TO WANT SOMETHING THAT YOU DON'T HAVE, THAN TO HAVE SOMETHING YOU DON'T WANT."

CONCLUSION

*D*espite the setbacks and brokenness of my past, I still believe the girl of my dreams is out there. I see her waiting for me to rescue her from her wilderness, and promise to love her forever. I can't explain how I know, but I know God has created a special lady for me. I can't tell you when I will find her. I can't tell you how I will find her. I can't tell you where I will find her. However, I can tell you that I will continue my search until at last I can say the words, "I Do," to the girl of my dreams before God and the world forever.

At the end of the day, in order to be happy, we must all come to the unshakable truth that God loves us and wants the best for us. Therefore, if we trust him and follow his plan for our lives, he has the power to supernaturally cause our paths to intersect with that special someone he has designed for each of us.

It is my prayer that as you read through this book, you found yourself falling deeper in love with Jesus Christ—and yourself. I hope you are starting to declare with unwavering conviction, "I am happily single and doing the work to prepare for my future." I will leave you with this final prayer.

A FINAL PRAYER FOR THE SINGLEHOOD JOURNEY

Dear God, I pray that you will carefully cover the love of my life. Lord, keep your arms of protection around the one you have destined for me. Preserve my love until our paths meet. Lord, I pray that you will allow the law of spiritual reciprocity to be kind to me. And, I pray that you will allow the law of harvest to remember my labor of love with my future spouse.

Lord, give us both the strength to be faithful in our singlehood as we prepare our hearts for each other. As a woman of God, I pray that you will prepare me to be my future husband's helper, hoverer, and healer. As a man of God, grant me the strength to become my future wife's pursuer, protector, and provider.

God, I now know what to do until I say, "I Do." I understand I must go through my personal Gethsemane moments just as my Jesus did. I must be willing to resolve within myself that your will is better than my will can ever be. Even in my deeper, darkest places of loneliness, I must be faithful to the plan that you have designed for my life.

So, Lord, hide my heart and my will in your hands until you reveal the love that is destined just for me. Dear God, grant me the patience, serenity, love, and wisdom to follow your will until my love's heart is given to me. Amen!

ENDNOTES

Chapter 2

1. *Merriam-Webster OnLine*, s.v. "detox," accessed June 17, 2017, http://www.merriam-webster.com/dictionary/detox.

Chapter 3

1. Thayer and Smith. "Greek Lexicon entry for Psuche" "The New Testament Greek Lexicon", accessed August 29, 2017. http://classic.studylight.org/lex/grk/view.cgi?number=5590.

Chapter 5

1. "That's not my job (poem)," Life Engineering, accessed October 20, 2017, http://life.engineering/thats-not-my-job-poem.

2. Lewis B. Smedes, "Forgiveness—The Power to Change the Past," *Christianity Today*, December 1 2002, http://www.christianitytoday.com/ct/2002/decemberweb-only/12-16-55.0.html.

Chapter 9

1. *Merriam-Webster OnLine*, s.v. "data," accessed August 29, 2017, http://www.merriam-webster.com/dictionary/data.

2. Nightingale, Earl. *Lead The Field*. Read by Earl Nightingale. Wheeling, IL: Nightingale-Conant, 2002. Audiobook, 4hrs.

3. Steven Covey, *The 7 Habits of Highly Effective People: Powerful Lessons in Personal Change* (New York: Free Press, 1989).

4. Marvin Gaye, vocal performance of "Let Your Conscience Be Your Guide," by Berry Gordy, recorded May 1961, on *The Soulful Moods of Marvin Gaye*, Tamla ⊢ T-54041, 45 rpm.

Chapter 10

1. "How we Absorb DNA via intercourse," Aether Force (blog), May 13, 2015, http://aetherforce.com/how-we-absorb-dna-via-intercourse

2. *Dictionary OnLine*, s.v. "x factor," accessed August 4, 2017, http://www.dictionary.com/browse/x--factor?s=t.

3. Michael Snyder, "19 Facts About Abortion In America That Should Make You Very Sick," The American Dream (blog), February 10, 2012, http://endoftheamericandream.com/archives/19-facts-about-abortion-in-america-that-should-make-you-very-sick.

4. Wess Stafford, "Divine Appointments," Compassion International (blog), June 18, 2012, https://blog.compassion.com/divine-appointments

5. Meg Jay, "The Downside of Cohabiting Before Marriage," *New York Times*, April 15, 2012

6. *Urban Dictionary OnLine*, May 8, 2017, s.v. "detox," accessed August 20, 2017, http://www.urbandictionary.com/define.php?term=soul+ties.

7. Nathaniel Hawthorne, *The Scarlet Letter* (Boston: Ticknor and Fields, 1850).

8. Good Reads, accessed August 20, 2017, https://www.goodreads.com/quotes/179066-a-man-must-be-big-enough-to-admit-his-mistakes

9. Smalley, Gary, "A Renewed Virginity," The Life Project (blog), July 12, 2017, https://thelife.com/a-renewed-virginity

ABOUT THE AUTHOR

*H*iawatha Hemphill is a minister, musician, trainer, and author. Educationally, he holds a B.A. from Livingstone College and an M.A.R. and M.Div. from Liberty University Rawlings School of Divinity. Other honors include citations from the Governor, Senate, and House of Representatives of the state of Hawaii.

Hiawatha is known for his unique ability to reach grassroots folks as well as intellectuals. He has ministered and trained throughout the United States, Canada, Mexico, and the Caribbean.

As a teacher and trainer, he has worked with the Winston Salem Forsyth County Schools, Rowan County Schools, Lynchburg City Schools, The Assurance Group, The National Black Child Institute and Skill Path.

Retired from the corporate world due to health issues, he services at Servant's Heart Worship Center located in High Point, NC. He is also a frequent guest panelist on the nationally televised program "Ask The Pastor" aired on the Total Christian Television Network.